WHY I WON'T HIRE BLACK PEOPLE

Racial Profiling for a Reason

Asa Leveaux

PHOENIX INK
NEW YORK

Copyright © 2013 by Asa Leveaux

All Rights Reserved. This publication is provided subject to the condition that it shall not, by way of trade or otherwise, be lent, resold, hired out or otherwise circulated without the author's prior written consent in any form of binding or cover. No part of this publication may be reproduced by any process, nor may it be stored in a retrieval system, transmitted or otherwise copied for public or private use without the written permission of the author. Although the author has made every reasonable attempt to achieve complete accuracy of the content in this article, he assumes no responsibility for errors or omissions. Use the information in this article at your own risk. Any trademarks, service marks, product names or named features are assumed to be the property of their respective owners, and are used only for reference. There is no implied endorsement if one of these terms is referenced in this book.

Publisher's Note: All stories and letters within are used by permission. All participants held the positions and job titles as noted at the time of correspondence.

ISBN: Ebook— 978-0-9885002-1-1
ISBN: Paperback— 978-0-9885002-3-5

Visit our Web site at www.whyiwonthireblackpeople.com

Printed in the United States of America

Contents

Dedication v
Acknowledgments vii
Letter to the Reader 1
Letter of Denial 15
Assessment #1: You have a victim's mentality 29
Assessment #2: You don't dress for success 45
Assessment #3: You do not possess a corporate
               appearance 59
Assessment #4: You are not respectful of time.....................75
Assessment #5: You do not understand networking
               principles..87
Assessment #6: You have a sense of entitlement...................99
Assessment #7: You lack professional communication
               skills..111
Assessment #8: You confuse attitude for strength 127
Assessment #9: You perpetuate negative stereotypes..........139
Assessment #10: You don't believe that you are amazing..151
Buried Treasure 163
APPENDIX A: Suggested Material......................................169
APPENDIX B: Success Stories 173

Dedication

This book is dedicated to those beautiful people who have been kissed by the sun and had once forgotten their worth and power.

Acknowledgments

Thank you to those in my vault who enable me to bear fruit that can nourish others, including: my mother, Noel Gray, who raised me to question and learn; my beautiful "sun" Adonis who makes everything better because I'm his Daddy; my siblings——Alicia, Ann, Henry and Chelsea——I thank you for having the courage to make me better. To my lover and friend Alexis——who would never allow me to feel anything but worthy to even consider a project of this magnitude. To my Kappa brothers Charles "Ceedy" Morgan, Tony Reames and the Oklahoma City Alumni Chapter of Kappa Alpha Psi Fraternity Incorporated; ——thanks for being truthful during this process. To Aundrae, Colleen, Brett, Rod, Eric, and Tekoya there are no words to what your friendship has meant to me over the years.

Thank you to those who shared their gifts and experiences that added to this project, including:

Diontae Allen, Lameka Grayson, Joseph Ballard, and Carolyn Madison who served as my editor. Thank you to those who have assisted with constructive feedback and provided the platforms and encouragement along the way allowing me to be in this moment, including: Millard Bruce, Beala Neel, Jill Gray, Robert Hayes, Devin Gonzales, Earl Lee, and Freida Johnson.

Thank you to the authors whose words have pierced my mind and showed me how instrumental books can be: Michael Eric Dyson, Dr. Cornel West, Touré, W.E.B DuBois, Malcolm Gladwell, Robert Kiyosaki, Eckhart Tolle, Napoleon Hill, Iyanla Vanzant, and Chaz Kyser.

Thank you to the musicians and singers who rocked my vision to existence on treble clefs and whole notes: Goapele, Incubus, Nina Simone, Jill Scott, Sade, Tupac, Kanye West, Jay-Z, The Foreign Exchange, Raheem Devaughn, Skrillex, Kindred Family Soul, Kem, The Clark Sisters, Travie McCoy, Dave Holister, Kem, Anita Baker, Swedish House Mafia, Adele, Maze featuring Frankie Beverly, Marvin Sapp, Mos Def, Tamela Mann, Rascal Flatts, Journey, Beres Hammond, and Timbalada.

Letter to the Reader

A letter to the people, love always

—Common

Dear Reader,

So the title has caught your attention, possibly stirred something within you, perhaps even gave you reason to be angry—great! This book is meant to identify reasons why Black people, especially our young Black people, are generally not hired at the same rate as our counterparts of other nationalities. I say "our" because I am a Black American.

As a Black American I have often been one of the few faces, sometimes the only face, with a dark complexion in a variety of settings. These places included the classroom, boardroom, executive meetings, and military briefings. As a Black American I was raised, educated, and played in suburban neighbourhoods outside of Oklahoma City, once commonly known to residents as "Murder 1," the "Panic Zone," and "Lloyd Ave." My upbringing was complete with Key Club meetings, wearing Band-Aids to school on certain colors of clothing to avoid gang affiliation, band practice, and possessing the ability to decipher corner-store graffiti. I was close enough to disparities that I could feel the effects but was protected enough that it wasn't allowed to consume me.

I have chosen to self-identify as being a Black American throughout this book. Globalization is not a term that is foreign to those in business, but rather a reality that is constantly etching closer to your doorstep. I say this to you because the term "African American" only refers to a specific group in the United States, which is another reason why my preference lies with self- identifying as being Black. This book is written not just for those who have been kissed by the sun in the United States, but rather for those who are experiencing distraction, discrimination, and distress while attempting to enter the corporate world.

Throughout this book you will also notice that I have made a conscious effort to capitalize the word Black when referring to those of African descent. In *Who's Afraid of Post-Blackness?* Michael Eric Dyson and Touré say it best: "I have chosen to capitalize the word "Black" and lowercase "white" throughout this book. I believe "Black" constitutes a group, an ethnicity equivalent to African-American, Negro, or in terms of a sense of ethnic cohesion, Irish, Polish, or Chinese. I don't believe that whiteness merits the same treatment. Most American whites think of themselves as Italian-American or Jewish or otherwise relating to other past connections that Blacks cannot make because of the familial and national disruptions of slavery. So to me, because Black speaks to an unknown familial/national past it deserves capitalization."

This book is also written for those who would like to increase their cultural intelligence. This impartation of Black culture will not include the Disney version of culture but rather the root of the issue. I say the *Disney version* because all too often we treat and view diversity as an amusement park or a world fair by consuming all the treats and what is most aesthetically pleasing to our senses. Instead, I will go to the root of the issue. This book will focus on notions of time, tolerance for change, communication styles, and varying attitudes by way of the Black collective consciousness and stereotypes.

At the age of twenty-two, I began my first official business venture, owning and operating a day-care center in Oklahoma. That was my first experience in searching for talent within the business world. Though I did hire many Black employees, I noticed that they did not operate the same way as their white counterparts, and the experiences were troubling at best. I am not saying that every Black person I hired did not do what she or he was hired to do—but those who did were the exception and not the rule. I have been a part of other business ventures, have had personal organizational successes, and have seen more Black Americans fall by the wayside during every facet of business. In this book, my intent is to identify the possible reasons for what others, including myself, have experienced in a way that is beneficial and direct.

The journey of *Why I Won't Hire Black People* began with a conversation with a mentor. I was honoured to be a part of a non-profit organization called American Corporate Partners. It is dedicated to assisting veterans in their transition from the armed services to the civilian workforce (for more information visit www.acp-usa.org). This is where I met a gift of a man who started the conversation about this topic in my mind. I was not excited before our first meeting because he was over fifty, Caucasian, and had never served in the Armed Forces. Though I was apprehensive, I am pleased that I did not allow myself to be dismayed by mere appearances. After getting to know one another over the course of a few mentoring lunches, he began to vocally ask, "Where were the others?" What he was asking was: where were the other young Black people who shared my drive and ambition? He did not ask in the way that I was used to, which would have been in a patronizing fashion, but rather an actual desire to meet others like me, or at the minimum, know that they existed. My first answer was an emphatic "everywhere," but as I began to think on the question in a bistro in Pasadena the reality began to develop like a Polaroid, and so did the questions.

As with most instances that I encounter, when I do not understand I began to ask questions. I started by asking my Black peers about the obvious lack of Black professionals. What I refer to as Black professionals are individuals of African descent who conduct themselves with pride and dignity in every aspect of their lives without the use of false intentions or practices. In response to the inquiry I was given every answer ranging from racist managements, failing education systems in black communities, the direct correlation between the increased incarceration rates of Black people, to the notion that our people are lazy. Though these answers had truth residing in them, I was not satisfied. I took the question a step further by asking white contemporaries in the different fields where I operate. To my chagrin, the answers were relatively the same with a few exceptions.

The statistics do nothing to inspire optimism for the young Black college graduate with a desire to enter the established corporate arena. Data from the Alliance for Board Diversity Report, a group comprised of organizations Catalyst, The Executive Leadership Council (ELC), The Hispanic Association on Corporate Responsibility (HACR), Leadership Education for Asian Pacifics, Inc. (LEAP), and The Prout Group, Inc. show that in 2010 white men dominated the boardroom of Fortune 500 companies by holding 74.5 percent of board seats; minority men held 9.9 percent; and minority women held 3 percent. Specifically, African-American women held 1.9 percent, while African-American men held 5.7 percent of these seats. The Economic Report of the President, published in February 2012, states "The unemployment rate for African Americans reached 16.7 percent in March 2010 and then again as recently as August 2011. The unemployment rates for Hispanics and African Americans as of January 2012 are well below their respective peaks—down 2.6 percentage points for Hispanics and 3.1 percentage points for African Americans—but still remain elevated" (p.166).

The statistics are not restricted to the United States. According to the Guardian (United Kingdom publication) there are unpublished government statistics that show unemployment for young Black male job seekers rose from 28.8 percent in 2008 to 55.9 percent in the last three months of 2011, twice the rate for young white people (9 March 2012 by James Ball, Dan Milmo and Ben Ferguson). The data was supplied by the Office for National Statistics (ONS), which did not include most students. Though the percentages are daunting, this is not meant to cause analysis paralysis. I challenge you, yes *you*, to digest these numbers without a desire to allow them to persist.

The intent of this book is also to assist Black people in understanding what it takes to enter the corporate world and what it takes to succeed within that world. Whether your aspirations consist of being a budget analyst for a defense contractor, a flight attendant, a personal assistant to a celebrity, owner of a janitorial company, or even the janitor, this book will give you the tools to operate within the parameters of professionalism. During these current economic times following the "Great Recession," finding employment can become a daunting task and could turn tumultuous if not equipped with the necessary knowledge and skills. By guiding you through the various reasons why I and others have not hired Black people, I hope to encourage you that it is time for action rather than accepting stagnation and negativity as a consequence of your blackness. My intent is not to validate prejudices against Black people. Prejudices arise from judgments that are preconceived or information that is limiting. This book will operate from neither. Though a few will see my approach as void of compassion or positivity, it comes from having been baptized in years of information and experience that has influenced my life in a personal way.

I have kept two things at the center of my focus during this project. The first and most important is to help you. All of my effort and efforts of those who have supported me will be in vain if you don't receive the help that is offered. To assist in ensuring that you gain practical information that you can use, I have given you space after each assessment to write down what you can do to become better. My second focus comes from the Arabian proverb that states, "The words of the tongue should have three gatekeepers: Is it true? Is it kind? Is it necessary?" This proverb has helped when I was concerned with mundane issues like word count and using certain experiences.

At this point you may still ask yourself why this book will be beneficial to your development. The reason is that I am a part of the generation that is currently in the initial search for jobs and careers or have finally realized what they really want to be when they grow up. Scholars and business executives who have been in their ivory towers for some time now write the majority of books on this subject. This diminishes their ability to fully grasp what is currently happening in the workplace. Nothing has been given to me. I have held positions ranging from a host at a twenty-four-hour diner, a factory worker mending textbooks, an employee at a fast-food restaurant (mopping floors to serving fries), and a plasma donor. I give those examples to say that no matter your present circumstance or position; there is more to you than what others and, more importantly *you*, see. This book was not created because of a school project or a forum discussion, but rather my life experiences. While you turn the next pages keep in mind that I want nothing more than what W.E.B. DuBois wrote in *The Souls of Black Folks,* which is to "to make it possible for a man to be both a Negro and an American, without being cursed and spit upon by his fellows, without having the doors of Opportunity closed roughly in his face."

Now a word about how this book is organized. It starts with a fictional letter of denial that was written by Diontae Allen. People usually don't get these or they receive form letters that do not give explicit reasons why employment was not offered. The letter provided is nothing like that; it is based on a real letter, based on various interviews that included everything that you will read. You'll say to yourself, "No wonder he didn't get the job!" But the behaviours he showed are just extreme (and in some cases not so extreme) versions of what my peers and I commonly see. It's these behaviours that hold Black people back; some of these are most likely holding you back. While reading the letter you may ask yourself the following: How could anyone conduct himself or herself in a job interview in this way? Why would anyone bother to write a letter to someone who acted like that? While you are reading ask yourself the following: *Am I that different? Would I do things that are similar, but less extreme?*

Afterwards, I describe in detail those behaviours. I tell you why they're harmful and why they'll keep you from success. It's hard to change behaviours, but you have to start somewhere, and that somewhere begins with under- standing. That's why I call each of these sections an "Assessment," and not a chapter. You need to understand in your heart—not just your head—what the problem is and why you need to change, which is why each assessment ends the way it does. If you fill those pages out as I ask you to, you'll start on a path to change.

At the conclusion I will cover the themes of this book again in a way that will bring the assessments together. My hope is that by that time you will have completed a portion of the Assessments so that you can begin to critique and evaluate yourself. The remainder of the book will give you resources to assist in what you should do next. Success stories from those who have been in your shoes are included. My fervent hope is that you will use them, and this book, to become the sort of Black person I, or anyone else, would insist on hiring

Letter of Denial

DO FOR SELF INCORPORATED
1234 MOTIVATION DR.

AMBITION, CA 54321

Dear Mr. Omar Pressed,

We are sending you this letter in regard to your recent inquiry and inter- view with our company Do For Self Inc. (D.F.S. Inc.). After deep consideration and much deliberation, we regret to inform you that we have decided to not take you on board. We are not usually in the habit of giving reasons for our denial of employment, however we have received an abundance of complaints from past interviewees of color stating we are a racist group, which I can assure you we are not.

I have received and reviewed the notes from your interview, and these were the few things that raised red flags for us.

Timeliness:

Your interview was scheduled for 9:30 AM Monday morning. My inter- viewer waited until

10:00 AM and was in the process of giving you a courtesy call when the pictures on his wall began to shake. To his surprise, he looked out of his window and saw you turning the corner a block away and pulling into our Human Resources office. You got out of your car and threw whatever you were smoking onto our sidewalk, and walked into the office. You approached the secretary at the front desk and reportedly said,

"Excuse me Miss Lady, I'm here for the interview I got."

She told you to be seated and to wait until you were called into the inter- viewer's office. I was informed that you introduced yourself as "O-Pressed" but your friends call you "O-Dawg." Mr. Pressed, this is a business and we only go by the name that is on our employee's identification card.

When the interviewer asked you the reason for your tardiness, you replied,

You know how it be brugh. C.P. time is in a different time zone. I had to make sure my gear was straight for this here interview.

That brings me to my next area of concern.

Appearance:

You came into our office with what seemed to be a nice collared shirt and a pair of khaki pants. The unlaced Nike shoes you had on were not so much an issue, as were the backside of your garments. The back of your shirt read *Sean Jean* across your upper back and *Hi Hater* across the lower. The collar of your shirt also read something but could not be seen due to your braided hair covering it. Though your un-tucked shirt hung down close to the back of your knees, the crotch of your pants was still visible because your pants hung far past your waistline. Your neck tie, which hung to the second button of your shirt, was nice; however the tie clamp (a pin of what seemed to be an AK-47), was not the image our company would like portrayed. Now we are in no way telling you how you can or should wear your clothing while in your element, but we here at D.F.S. adhere to a strict dress code of the utmost professionalism. Customer service is the tool that drives and keeps this company far ahead of its competition.

That brings me to my next area of concern.

Vocabulary Skills:

As stated previously, we here at D.F.S. Inc, are a very customer-service driven corporation. From the notes in the interview, you seem to lack the necessary vocabulary skills needed to accomplish our company's intent. When asked whether you had any prior experience in this field, you answered,

Nah, not really. But I'm real adaptative to whatever situation I be put in. You aint got no job I can't do yo. I put in all kinda work on the street, but aint nothing I can really say to you. Feel me dog?

Mr. Pressed, though we do admire your drive, and somewhat "can-do" attitude, what you've done on the street is irrelevant to the needs of this company. You lack the vocabulary skills needed to be successful in this company. We deal with customers on a daily basis at high volumes throughout each and every day. On your application in the "*Languages*" section, you stated that you spoke both *English* and *Ebonics*. We were unsure whether you wrote this in a joking manner, which if it was, we in no way find it humorous. In the event that this was a serious entry on your part, we again regret to inform you that Ebonics is:

1. Not a language accepted by any respectable company, and 2. Not a language that the majority of our customers speak. So this "skill" of yours would be of no use to our mission. I'm certain that no school in our immediate district has Ebonics in any textbook in their library.

That brings me to my last area of concern.

Educational Background:

When asked by the interviewer what level of education you've reached, you stated,

Man I tried that whole school thing, but it wasn't for a brother like me. I got all the way up to the ninth grade and this white teacher always was on my case tryna make it hard for ya boy. I said that mess is for the birds so I skated out on 'em. The rest of my educational experience was out there in them streets, ya dig? I just tried the whole GED thing, but all that reading and studying is for suckas so I stopped going. Plus I needed some paper and that's why I'm up in here tyrna get on wit yall. I was gon join the Army but I aint for the white man tryna tell me what to do all the time. Feel me?

Mr. Pressed, we are very aware that school is not the only place to learn life lessons, and there is more to life than education. However, education is what sets you apart from your peers in times such as this. I am also aware that college is not for everyone, but there are an abundance of other trade and vocational schools you could attend that would be more tailored to your person. Do you know how you hide important life secrets from fools? -You put them in books. Now, I am in no way calling you a fool, but if before you came in to your interview, you had picked up a book on the interview process, or maybe consulted with someone in a business profession, you may have gotten further in our interview process. On the contrary, you relied on your street knowledge and slick tongue, which has probably gotten you far outside in the streets, but will more than likely get you nowhere in the workforce. You may be very persuasive and have sharp wit—skills that are much needed in our company— but without the credentials to back them, you are just another person in the selection pool.

In closing, I would like to share a bit about myself, and talk to you on a more personal note.

Now this may come as a shock to you given your "O-Pressed" mentality, but I am not a person of pale pigmentation. I am an educated Black man who had drive and goals from the day I set foot in school. What also may come as a shock is that I looked into your file, and recognized you from junior high and high school. We attended the same classes from seventh to the ninth grade. I remember the first day of high school when you came reeking of the same cannabis you reportedly smelled of during the interview. That came as a shock to me, seeing as how you had such high marks in junior high. The two guys that you were so close to seemed to have had a huge impact on your post junior-high change.

It was around the time the movie *Malcom X* hit the theaters, and I remember you always talking about how the "white man" is trying to hold us back, and the teachers were a part of this "System" put in place to keep a foot on the necks of people of color. That teacher you spoke of in the interview, Mr. Hardlove, was also a teacher of mine. You weren't the only one whose case he was on. He was constantly on mine as well. I, however, took a different approach to his means of teaching. I looked at him as a challenge and a roadblock that I was determined to get over. Do you know that he stood there waiting for me to cross that stage on graduation day with a smile that could only come from a proud parent? He told me this:

I push the ones who I know will succeed in life. They are the ones I take special interest in; I give them the hardest time. That is not to be cruel to them. It is my way of preparing them for the challenges ahead in life. Nothing will be given to you. You have to make every path, and stay on it. The ONLY person who can hold you back is YOU.

I took those words of encouragement as fuel to a fire already lit. From the day I could walk, I was surrounded by bad influences and temptations that I had to struggle daily to resist. Living in a single parent home, like you, I wanted to get a job and help out with the bills, which I did, resulting in a drop in my grade point average. Still driven to go to college despite the lack of scholarship, I worked my entire college career in order to pay for tuition. Those were the hardest days of my life, but I made my path and stuck to it. When my college professors told me that college was not for me, I refused to let them get in my way. The only person who could hold me back was I. I graduated and started this business from the ground up. The name, "Do For Self " is pretty much self-explanatory.

Please don't take this as me claiming to be better, or even smarter than you are. I in no way think you are dumb. The secretary at the front desk informed me that while waiting, you assembled a puzzle on the desk that myself and colleagues have been trying to put together for months, as well as all the Chinese wooden mechanical puzzles. I was told that after your interview, as you were walking back to your car, you stopped and helped one of my employees who had been having engine trouble. She has been to work on time every day since you left because of it.

With that being said, you are not worthless. You have skills necessary in the workforce that far surpass that of a "street pharmacist." Stop blaming the "white man" for all of your shortcomings, and take responsibility for self.

You would think that with me sharing this story and our mirrored back- ground that it would end in me "giving" you the opportunity to prove yourself in my company. I would be remiss to do so. My decision to not take you on is a page taken straight out of Mr. Hardlove's book. Nothing will be given to you in this life. You make your path and you stick to it. I can only hope that you take these words as guidance and encouragement, and not a foot to your neck. Good luck in all of your future endeavours Mr. Pressed, and always remember, "The only person who can hold you back is *you*."

Very Respectfully,
D. Termand
CEO, Do For Self Inc.

Though this letter is fictional the situation has replayed over and over, again and again. Everything Omar Pressed did here held him back, kept him from getting a job he could do, and kept him from success. He could stay with this feeling of being unsuccessful temporarily or permanently, depending on what he does next. In the next sections of this book I'll point out behaviors that hold Black people back, including some that may possibly be holding you back. You may feel angry or

uncomfortable. That's good; I'm getting through to you. Growth is not always enjoyable—hence the term "growing pains." As you continue to read the following pages and feel uncomfortable, stop and think: *Who is the real target for my anger? Can I do better? Who is putting me in a place that makes me angry?* Most of the time it will be you—not me.

Assessment #1

YOU HAVE A VICTIM'S MENTALITY

You is kind, you is smart, you is important.

—The Help

It would be wrong to not begin tis discussion without presenting the history that has caused such an unlevel playing field in the United States. The point of this section is not to make excuses (which I believe re tools of the incompetent) for the lack of effort of some individuals, but purely to state the facts. Roughly twelve million Africans were brought to the "new world", beginning with the Spanish. Jamestown, the first successful English colony in what became the United States, was the first one to have Africans as slaves. Of course the practice affected the continent of Africa, but it also affected the way the world has regarded African descendants—both historically and presently. Maulana Karenga, in *Effects on Africa*, spoke of slave trade: "The morally monstrous destruction of human possibility involved redefining African humanity to the world, poisoning past, present and future relations with others who only know us through this stereotyping and thus damaging the truly human relations among people of today."

This cruel and profitable exploitation persisted for centuries, beginning as indentured servitude and resulting in brutal practices that included shackling, hanging, beating, mutilation, branding, breeding, rape, kidnapping, separation of family members, which were all common and legal. The atrocities suffered by men, women, and children of African descent are so varied and complex that attempting to lay out the history with the reverence required of such a task is beyond the scope of this book. However, I will note that the way a person (or in this case a people) is treated and mistreated is indicative of how they feel about and value themselves. Anyone who has gone through a basic training program in a military capacity understands this phenomenon. It is the job of the drill instructor to tear you down until you lose any identity that is not in line with the values of the military. Unlike slavery, the military program builds you again with integrity, a value system, a sense of contributing to a greater good, and a posture of honour.

When you consider finding employment, starting a family, or making any other major life decisions, it is important to know that it all begins with the mind. The wrong mindset can derail your pursuit of an endeavour. Slavery has caused a virtual chain to persist in the minds of a number of Black people. We tend to believe that we are not good enough, our presence is not valued, and our potential is stifled. This endangers the destiny of many.

Reasons for this mental state have been approached in many avenues including scholarly written work, news commentary and radio talking points. I do not wish for this book to be a reawakening of past hurts; it is now time to reveal a new story. A new story is needed because many Black people are addicted to those stories from our past—and continuing to focus on them has not served us well. We know about slave auctions separating family members with the strike of a gavel, being legally considered less than a complete person, vicious attacks—and many other injustices. Post-traumatic stress from our past-is ingrained within our collective memories—and we digest it on a daily basis. I wish to take our quilted history and thread a new story that will help us look toward the possibilities of the future.

It is now time to reinvent and relish a new story worthy of our addiction—a story of promise and hope fuelled by education and persistence. That is the mentality that we need. Dr. John Ogbu, a Professor at the Department of Anthropology at the University of California in Berkeley, California, gives four reasons why Black Americans continue to have collective status problems: involuntary incorporation into society, instrumental discrimination, social subordination, and expressive mistreatment. These reasons are also due to "dominant group members stigmatize(ing) minorities' food, clothing, music, values, behaviours, and language or dialect as bad and inferior to theirs."

Having a victim's mentality can and will keep you from finding employment and from achieving corporate success once you are hired. I have witnessed many African Americans who have blamed white management for things that were outlined in the employee handbook. For example, if the policy states that vacation time may not be given during the probationary period and you decide to request off for a culturally significant event, then the blame lies solely on you. A defeatist mentality arises when you allow your- self to think that because you could not take part in a culturally significant event, your culture is now being disregarded as it was for those ancestors. A victim's mentality, in this context, can stem from a slave's mentality. A slave's mentality was one where a master or overseer told the slave what to do daily. Slaves were not there to think because their thoughts were not valued. Slaves did not show any initiative because that was not their job or what they were created for. Slaves did not give unwarranted input because the taskmaster did not realize that the slave had the mental capacity to manage more effectively.

Have you really been that brainwashed into believing that your dreams are not possible, that you cannot be hired, that your skills are not valued because of the color the creator painted you? If you have allowed your mind to succumb to this untruth, it is my greatest intent that you allow your mind to be changed.

Beverly Tatum speaks about a concept known as internalized oppression in her book *Why Are All the Black Kids Sitting Together in the Cafeteria?* This concept refers to members of a stereotyped group internalizing the images and references that they have encountered over time. This can be detrimental to a person, providing him with a multitude of reasons to think that he cannot become everything that he is destined to be. For example, based on what is readily available and popular on television, a Black young lady around the age of eleven, might think the following about herself: that she should "shake what her mama gave her" in an effort to get cash, that she should not find it absurd if she does not know who the father of her child is, that Black women in power do not exist, and that being connected to a Black man of substance would require marrying a president.

When you pursue employment and accept a job offer you can sabotage your own success by allowing all of your experiences of oppression (including collective experiences) to make you uncomfortable, untrusting, and skeptical of people you work for and with. For example, when you first meet the person who will interview you, she may make a comment about your hair. Your experience combined with the collective experience automatically may put your mind and body in a defensive state. You may be ready and willing to justify your role as the beautifully-made African queen or king that you know you are regardless of how the media displays what beauty is via relaxed hair and bleaching creams. However, the interviewer's comments were harmless and actually were meant to be a compliment, but because you constantly struggle with internalized oppression, the interview becomes tense and unproductive.

Let's discuss a scenario involving a Black female chaplain assistant during her first days interning at a retirement community. In order for this chaplain assistant to possess such a title she has to ensure she has acquired a Master of Divinity degree along with other certifications—with the added benefit of being hired by the department. During a typical day at the retirement community, she has failed to take initiative regarding the members of the community needing spiritual care. When approached as to why she did not take initiative, she responded that no one told her to perform that particular task, even though she understood that it needed to be done. You may agree with her notion of not doing anything without being told but I would ask, *why*. At her level of responsibility, education, and experience, people would not perceive her as a farm hand who needs to be told to collect eggs for the day. Most would agree that a chaplain's assistant is expected to perform duties that are not outlined in the job description but that would add value to the nature of the position, which is commonly known as an *implied task*.

An *employee's* mentality is one of self-worth and self-value. It is important that you realize that a company saw the value embedded within you to allow you to join their organization. As a Black person it will be more common to work in a place where other Black faces are sprinkled throughout the organization, which can make you feel isolated. It is important that you walk in on the first day knowing what you bring to the table in spite of and including the color of your skin. If you go into the workplace with thoughts that your presence does not matter, based entirely on speculation, eventually it won't.

Many people see their value in terms of monetary compensation. However, Black people have been receiving the short end of the payroll stick since the days that followed the Emancipation Proclamation. Newly emancipated slaves and freeman where paid three dollars less on average than were their white counter- parts in the Union Army. However, just as we did then, we endure and strive because we know there is a little Black boy or girl out there in the world who will need our assistance when feeling what you have felt. Another reason why it is important to know your value is so you don't allow yourself to be placed in a position or organization that does not meet the standard that you constantly represent. I can understand if you are college student and are working as a part-time employee at a local foundation doing menial tasks, but if you have received your master's degree in Hospitality Management then accepting a night auditor position at a motel will likely be a step in the wrong direction. The pain you feel as a victim can serve as a boost into your destiny. I have pursued modeling since the first time I overheard a girl say, "oh, he cute" in that way Oklahoma girls can say such a thing. I have experienced a gamut of things in that endeavor from being in fashion shows, working with European photog- raphers, and being appreciated for the work I have done as a whole. I have come across "critics" in the modeling industry who have said the following: "You are too short."; "Your skin color is not marketable."; "Come back when you grow into the height requirement—"; and "I hope you aren't pursuing this professionally." To anyone, model or not, those statements can be damaging to the psyche and ultimately deter a person from a goal. Fortunately, what it instilled in me was a deeper bond with my goal. As far as critics go, I allow critics to be just that, critics. The best quote I've ever heard that may help you is, "What other people think of you is none of your business."

The way you believe in yourself sets the standard for everyone around you and those you come in contact with. You have to think you are capable of being an executive assistant, logistics manager, or systems analyst. Your thoughts are more important than you may know. Everything that you want in life and desire for your life begins with a thought. Your thoughts become things, and those things are the tools that you can build your life with.

So you have a *victim's* mentality. You may call it a chip on your shoulder or "that's how I am," but the bottom line is that your actions are in response to the actions of others. The rudeness you display is falsely disguised as strength. You have the ability to change this today—now—*right now*. Do not allow your success to be dictated by the negative story that you keep repeating to your- self constantly. You may even say that not everyone has someone in his or her corner. If that is your case, then let me reintroduce myself as the "corner boy" (person in your corner) and your personal hype man. While we haven't yet met, know I love you and that there is power in your ability to do the greatest things imaginable. You are a bright star in this world and the next. There is more to you than what others see, and now it is time to wash yourself, iron your clothes, spray on the smell-good, and embody the successful individual that you are!

WHAT CAN I DO TO BECOME BETTER?

Each evening spend fifteen minutes thinking about the day. When did you display a victim's mentality? What caused you to do that? How did it hold you back? How could you have handled the situation so you would not have acted like, and thus been a victim? What will you do differently in the future?

Keep this record every workday or every day that you are searching for employment for an entire week. Then review it before you begin each week. See where you have improved and identify habits that you still need to change.

1. _____

_____

_____

_____

2. _____

_____

_____

___

3. ___

___

___

___

4. ___

___

___

___

5. ___

___

___

___

Assessment #2

YOU DON'T DRESS FOR SUCCESS

You cannot climb the ladder of success dressed in the costume of failure.

—Zig Ziglar

What did you wear to work yesterday? What did you wear on your last job interview? What are you wearing right now? I ask you these questions because the way people initially respond to you has a great deal to do with the way you are dressed. When we meet a potential mate or go to interviews we usually come prepared to introduce *our representative*. Our representative is the one we use on our daily campaign trail of life. We use these representatives in our professional and personal lives. When I campaign to meet a potential mate or employer, I am precise in my endeavour. I understand that women may think a certain way because of anecdotal information given from their mothers and/or friends, which may include "only date a man who takes care of his feet because on his worst day he will treat you as good as his most neglected body part." I am also aware that supervisors, in their years of experience, come to find that if an employee ensures that his outer appearance is handled with care then he may more often take that same care with tasks and customers. So to avoid problems, I make it a priority that my feet are properly groomed daily and that my shoes are always in good shape. I look over my clothing from collar to cufflink. Your representative displays on the outside what you feel is the most positive reflection of you and what others will respond to positively. Before discussing appropriate dress for the office, it is important to under- stand the word *conservative*. The word *conservative* is an adjective that means in favour of preserving existing conditions—cautious, traditional. In my letter to you, I laid out that white men currently manage the corporate world, which makes them the deciders of existing conditions. You can be angry with this and may want to rebel against the status quo because of your need to be an individual so that you can "express yourself." The bottom line is that being able to express yourself is a wonderful thing that many people are able to do, but no matter how valued that may be it doesn't pay the rent. Black people are a group that includes fashion-forward individuals and sects that revel in various expressions of dress. These cultural assets, however redeeming, will not suffice in a majority of corporate settings. Sects that include hip-hop, Pentecostal church people, hipsters, skaters, and other groups that portray varied forms of casualness are what to separate from, in part, when presenting yourself as a viable candidate.

When interacting with peers, potential investors, or supervisors you want to ensure that your dress is one that matches your skills and where you want to aspire. The common thought about this is that you dress and present your- self two levels up from where you currently are or are applying. This allows a physical transformation in the minds of others and yourself to envision where you are vertically headed. For instance, if you have received a position at an accounting firm as a mail handler but you wish to be a Certified Public Accountant (CPA), then don't come to the workplace in Sketchers, skinny jeans, and designer t-shirts. Instead come to the office in a pair of fitted slacks, a shirt with a collar that is tucked in with a belt, and shoes that were not meant for skateboarding or planking. Show them that your representative is really an accountant, not a mail clerk. If you treat yourself as an accountant, in time everyone else there will too.

I am a product of the Church of God in Christ in the Southeast Jurisdiction of Oklahoma. My formative years were spent watching my father serving bishops by hand and foot and giving "popcorn sermons" where ministers were given five minutes to deliver a sermon in an effort to hone his craft. I saw my mother teach everything from Sunshine Band and Y.P.W.W (Young People Willing Worker) and donning her white uniform on every first Sunday as she assisted in communion. My grandmother, a seamstress, was known for her "church hats" and the ability to make a robe fit for the most prestigious of pulpits. I was amazed every year I attended the Holy Convocation in Memphis, TN, not only because I was able to miss school, but also because of the fashion show that strutted, switched, and swayed before my eyes in the 1990s. Holy Convocation was the original Project Runway. The dress worn by many parishioners of historically black churches is authentic and cannot be duplicated. However, these garments work only in their original intended settings. I cringe when I enter a bank, administration office, or local business and see a suit that summons songs sung by gospel singer, Dottie Peoples. When Black people wear such clothes, they are telling everyone that they are outsiders who don't belong in banks and businesses. The fact is that you don't gain the same initial and continuous level of respect that your position is inclined to have when your dress shoes look like Skittles and your blouse is bedazzled. In the corporate world, it is your results rather than your plumage that should garner recognition.

I know that I have to explain to you the image I have chosen for this book of a young minority male sagging in jeans. If you are reading this book, I suspect that you are past the sagging stage and do not want to be associated with such a practice. However, the truth remains that this mental picture is associated with Black youths. Some of you may be unaware of the origins of sagging. It comes from rules set in prison where inmates are not allowed belts, so their pants must sag. Another aspect is that inmates could signal their homo- sexual preferences by allowing their pants to worn below the waist. Black males are overrepresented in the United States prison system; once these inmates are released from prison and return home, these prison habits are difficult to break.

When you wear sagging pants you're creating a representative that says, "I'm a criminal" or at least may become a criminal. Is that the way you want to present yourself? Is that what you truly are? Is that what you strive to become? Many other people, including white people, know what sagging pants mean. But even those who don't can read the body language that is often associated with it and the message it sends—even if you don't realize it.

When I was in junior high and high school sagging was specifically written into the dress code policy and was grounds for suspension. I have never under- stood the perceived appeal of sagging and can admit that judgmental thoughts cross my mind whenever I see someone who chooses to wear their clothes in such a way. It's such an issue that transit agencies, airlines, and even presidential candidates have something to say with regards to that fashion. In 2008 presidential candidate Barack Obama appeared on MTV and gave an exclusive interview with Sway Calloway about the issue.

Barack Obama stated, "Having said that, brothers should pull up their pants. You're walking by your mother, your grandmother, and your underwear is showing. What's wrong with that? Come on. There are some issues that we face that you don't have to pass a law [against], but that doesn't mean folks can't have some sense and some respect for other people. And, you know, some people might not want to see your underwear—I'm one of them."

Ladies, when dressing for the workplace less does not equate to more. Having grown up with a mother who was constantly on my three sisters about their dress I have the benefit and curse of knowing when a female is not up to standard. Everything ranging from the proper use of a slip, to quality stockings, girdle usage, and what you should look like in a properly fitted brassiere is something that I can notice within the first moments of an introduction. But I'm not alone. Many people who will interview you for jobs can do the same thing. You will find assistance in the appendixes that I have provided for you, but there are some basics to being properly dressed. If you look in the mirror and the first thing that you see is cleavage, then please find another blouse. Also, it is a good rule that while you are still in the comforts of your home do a dress rehearsal when wearing an ensemble for the first time. For instance, if you commonly reach for things on shelves, bend over frequently, or climb stairs or step ladders, do those things to see how your clothing will respond to those demands.

Men, what we have to understand is that just because we do not have vast department store floors dedicated to us does not mean that we should present ourselves with any less care and attention. All too often colleagues think that they have to be dressed by Alan Flusser in order to be seen as fashion-forward at work. The intent is to find the middle ground so that you do not become bankrupt because of purchases while still remembering that Dickies are not dress pants. Faux pas that are common and that can be fixed with little effort besides attention to detail include the following: ensuring that your clothing is free of stains and wrinkles before you leave your home; ensuring that your clothes still fit in a way that your buttons and zippers are not visibly fighting for custody or that it looks as though you are wearing your big brother's clothes. Items that are faded do not add to your persona but rather your lack of self-respect. I am not delusional about the price of clothes that meet the standard. I have been a long-time benefactor of second-hand retail and discount clothing stores. More often than not I can adequately dress myself for around $50 or less by simply taking the time, since money may not be abundant.

So what are some items that you can acquire to ensure that you can "look like a bag of money" the way Rick Ross raps about? When I am asked this question my answer is to start with basics. The basics include a good pair of black shoes, a button-down collared white shirt or blouse, a black belt to match your shoes, a black, navy, or grey blazer, and a pair of slacks that are as close to being tailored as you can find from the rack. The next thing you want to do is observe your environment. All dress is not conducive to your respective workplace. Just as it would not be proper to wear tennis shoes working as an estate planner, it would also not be adequate to wear designer scarves working as a carpenter, or pumps if you are a warehouse worker. It is important that you dress in a conservative fashion that does not bring any unwarranted attention.

The interview is a formal meeting and should be treated as such. The only reason to not dress formally is if you received information from the individual interviewing you or the hiring department has contacted you and instructed you to dress in a different way i.e. business casual. Please note that just because you are interviewing at a call center where the dress code is considerably relaxed, it is still appropriate to dress formally. There are those positions such as bank teller, receptionist, executive assistant, or public relations representative that require you to work with the clients of the company more frequently, which will make you subject to more scrutiny about the way you dress and present yourself.

WHAT CAN I DO TO BECOME BETTER?

As you go about your day, think about the way you view people according to how they are dressed as well as how people respond to you according to yours. Does their dress make you feel comfortable or defensive? What part of their clothing could be changed to make you feel more secure? Do you receive better treatment when you wear certain clothes?

At the end of each day this week, think about your representative. How did you clothe yourself? Did your clothing match the places where you want to work, or did it make you stick out? Did you look like someone who could be a worker there, or did you look like a Black person who was just visiting?

1. _____

_____

_____

_____

2. _____

3. _____
_____
_____

4. _____
_____
_____
_____

5. _____
_____
_____
_____

Assessment #3

YOU DO NOT POSSESS A CORPORATE APPEARANCE

You could be a fuckin' accountant, not a dope dealer.

—Tupac Shakur

I am the oldest of five children who were born and raised in Oklahoma City, Oklahoma. In recent years, a younger sibling was going through a transition phase, stuck between two realms. She did not know whether she wanted to be part of the streets, with all of the excitement and lack of responsibility that it brought, or to pursue her college education and be a productive citizen. She didn't decide until another sibling and I told her we could not allow her to act this way and to constantly embarrass herself and our family. That information was hard for her to swallow. We were raised to be thick-skinned and powerfully blunt, but we were apprehensive about revealing the truth to her.

This story shows what happens in the workforce. When employers are screening your application, résumé, and you, they want to make sure that selecting you will not embarrass them. There are both subtle and blunt ways that they look at things to reach their conclusion. A subtle way may be noticing the use of explicit music on your cell phone. If someone calls you for an interview that could very well cost you a position. Or they might notice that you have showed up to an interview with a visible wristband from the nightclub you attended the night before. A blunt example would be the way you treat the receptionist at the front desk or a resume that is not formatted or is dirty or wrinkled.

You may be unsure about the difference between dressing for success and possessing a corporate appearance. That may be because both descriptions have been used to discuss attire that is suitable for the workplace. Appearance not only deals with your selection of clothing but also the scents you use, your natural body odor, your hairstyle choice, the offensiveness of your breath, use of makeup, and exposed tattoos. Private schools that have mandatory uniforms and the military are excellent examples of the differences between dress and appearance. It is common to see a newly enlisted soldier "look" like a newly enlisted soldier. Though the individual has on the same uniform as their superior, you can often identify who is who with a blink of an eye. For instance, new recruits often walk in a way that is not seen in experienced soldiers, which includes walking slowly (known as walking without a sense of purpose), walking with a limp or possessing a stride that exemplifies a person who has not identified with their purpose.

In any metropolitan area or large city you will likely find two streets: Main Street and Martin Luther King Blvd. These two streets differ aesthetically as well as with regard to population. Common sites on Main Street, which you can find in any town in the United States, would include the following: respected banks; retail establishments; and people walking in business attire and moving about with intentionality. The location serves as a central location for socializing. What you can expect from Martin Luther King Blvd, in any city in the United States, are check cashing business, gun stores, liquor stores, fast food and soul food restaurants, businesses void of continuous improvements, and Pentecostal places of worship.

I bring this up because of a reality that my Black peers and I have recognized. It is common for people of color to be employed in a sanitized area of their city because they are on a career path. Then, as the weekend nears they turn their sights on the Eastside, or College Park or Oak Cliff—all of which are known as "the black sides of town" in Oklahoma City, Atlanta, and Dallas respectively. The dichotomy of acceptable appearances, according to what street you are on, is something that you may regard as threatening to your authentic self. However, if you look at this differently you may see that it serves as a way to express yourself in more ways than one.

Celebrity fashion stylist Rachel Zoe has said, "Style is a way to say who you are without having to speak." I agree with Ms. Zoe and use this thought when considering what my appearance will be at any location. Growing up I was known as the "church boy" or a "preppie." I identified with starched polos from the local Goodwill and Cole Haans. However, as I have grown and matured I have been able to master my personal compartmentalization of my appearance. What I mean by this is that I now allow myself to operate within subcultures as I see fit. For instance, you can catch me on Venice Beach with skinny jeans, Vans, and a graphic tank. While attending church service with family members I find Stacy Adams and paisley neckties to be the norm. While attending a conference or business lunch my use of colors and scents are minimized so as not to distract from my contributions and successes that I want to speak for me. For the most part, no one is intentionally trying to turn you into a mind- less corporate sheep that is void of individualism but rather wanting to give you the skill to be able to wear what is appropriate in every instance.

Hiring managers, human resource assistants, and recruiters have noticed that young Black men and women believe that they should be regarded as qualified candidates even though they fail to comply with standards that have been established. For instance, baggy jeans, t-shirts, hooded sweatshirts, short shorts, outlandish hair designs (including coloring), tennis shoes, excessive jewelry, and tank tops are perfectly fine for casual activities focused on relaxation and fun, but they are not worthy of being taken seriously in an office setting. Also, you must understand the connotation that your desired appearance has for other people. I am the furthest thing from a thug, but if I am on the train with pants that are sagging (which is nothing more than paying homage to prison culture) with my underwear visible, an oversized jersey, and a beanie cap, I have to understand the feelings that I inflict on society. The feelings have only a portion to do with the skin that you are in. There are a disproportioned number of violent crimes being done by young Black youths dressed in the fashion just described. If you dress that way, you may become a poster-child for violence that is already etched in the minds of many. To avoid this, I suggest that you change your appearance when you expect a different perception result. Please note that I said *change your appearance*, which is not synonymous with changing who you are. You are so much more than hoodies, shoes, and chains.

Paying attention to how you appear to customers, peers, and supervisors throughout the course of your day is highly important, though you don't want to forget to dress your avatar. Not only are you on constant display but also so is your social media profile. Whether you are on Facebook, MySpace, LinkedIn, Twitter, or Google+ you should actively manage the images of you that are available on the Internet. If you have visited career blogs or articles on the topic of getting your first job in the last year, then you know about the seriousness of protecting your online image.

Employers, now more than ever, will search for what you do on a daily basis to give them more insight as to what type of employee you will be for their organization. I have decided to not hire people based on profile pictures alone. For example, I have seen young women with bongs in their pictures and young men with sexually explicit quotes and/or pictures. With the way social media sites are taking positive steps regarding your privacy options, there isn't any reason that I should know how scandalous you were in Miami or Dubai. Though others and I understand that there are different facets to all people, you want to be vigilant as to which facet is being reflected to society. Employers don't have the luxury of knowing about the sum of all things that make you the person you are today, so assist them in what you would like them to know first and only.

After the destruction of the World Trade Center on September 11, 2001 Muslim Americans were perceived to be nothing more than murderers who were planning their next attack. Many of us still see this as a possibility and are heightened to great extremes when in an airport witnessing Middle Easterners at the same gate. I must say that when I see someone in traditional Arab garb boarding the same airplane my first reaction is one of fear, and one that I am not proud of having. I mention this confession of profiling because it is legitimized in hiring practices and not just among white, middle-aged men. There are business standards that people in every race, including Black people, succumb to and will expect for you to adhere to. It would be naïve of you to walk into a Black-owned establishment and expect an entrepreneur to allow you to interact with the customer base that has taken her years to build with an appearance that is below the operating standard or that can be described as "trifling" on the sole basis of you both sharing the same pigment. Just as I felt uncomfortable about being aboard an airplane with people of Middle Eastern descent, business owners will cringe at the idea of employing someone whom they can smell before they can see.

When speaking about corporate appearance, it has been my experience that women have the most to gain and lose. To err on the side of caution, it is a best practice to appear more conservative than your peers. All too often, in various settings and career fields, I have witnessed women allowing events to undermine their business sense in an effort to show their "wild side."

During my employment with a defense contractor, I was invited to the company Christmas party (not a holiday party but a real-life Christmas party). I was accustomed at that point to seeing these educated women on a daily basis update project managers, spearhead quality analysis on departments, and give cost comparisons on spreadsheets that would boggle the novice mind. What I witness that evening placed some of their accomplishments on the backburner to what I view as "industry cleavage." It is not my intention to sound or appear sexist by any means, but I will not give women a pass on what is acceptable at a company-sponsored function that takes place away from the workplace. I don't want you to fall into the trap of letting your guard down because of the inclination that you think you can. My advice for you in this context is to feel free to go to the company event and have an enjoyable time getting to know your peers and those senior to you without the strains of the daily grind. However, keep in mind that you do not want to be the one that is being whispered about before the Monday morning budget meeting.

In preparation for writing this book I visited http://implicit.harvard.edu to take their Implicit Association Test (IAT) on race. That particular IAT "requires the ability to distinguish faces of European and African origin. It indicates that most

Americans have an automatic preference for white over black." I had read the first-hand accounts of different people who had taken this test and was certain that I could, with a good amount of certainty, project the outcome. However, that is not what happened. My result stated, "Your data suggest a slight automatic preference for European American compared to African American." Even though I took the test more than once I am partial to faces of European origin or as my college friend says, I love pink people. How could this be? Am I subconsciously a self-hating Black man? Has society bamboozled me?

Jay-Z has stated, "I've never looked at myself and said that I need to be a certain way to be around a certain sort of people. I've always wanted to stay true to myself, and I've managed to do that. People have to accept that." You may also think that it is no use to change who you are just to get a paycheck and that it would make you a sell-out. You do not need to sell-out but rather attain more. Attain more knowledge that allows you to operate in unfamiliar worlds. Jay-Z knows this as well, which is why when Anthony DeCurtis interviewed him he said, "With education comes refinement."

If I walked into your workplace could I tell what position you held just by your appearance? Based on your demeanor throughout the day would I acknowledge that you have a great temperament for your job and for your co-workers? These questions may prompt a revelation for you, but if you consider these consistently then revelation will turn into routine. Your routine will be sure to catch the attention of your superiors as well. It is a common reality in the workplace that office appearances become more formal with seniority. If your goal is to grow with this company it would be wise to present yourself in a way to have your peers and supervisors see you in a light set aside for your next level.

WHAT CAN I DO TO BECOME BETTER?

While you run errands to the bank, school, place of worship, or shopping mall, take one minute before you enter and think about what you expect for the employees to wear while offering services and what you would do if this expectation were not met. Then think about your appearance. Does it match how you want to be seen? If you had to be one of the employees you meet on your errands, could you present the right appearance?

1. _____

   _____

   _____

   _____

2. _____

   _____

   _____

   _____

3. _____

_____

_____

_____

4. _____

_____

_____

_____

5. _____

_____

_____

_____

Assessment #4

YOU ARE NOT RESPECTFUL OF TIME

I want to show them the difference between what they think you are and what you can be.

—Ernest J. Gaines, *A Lesson Before Dying*

I could not begin this conversation without addressing the dreadful and ever-present "CP time" reference. Most of you already know that CP is an acronym for colored people. CP time is used to trivialize the way some African Americans are habitually late. Some actually suggest that C.P.T. is the official time zone in which Black people operate. I remember hearing this reference from family members at an early age and was not amused then as I am not amused now.

When attending any event that dealt with a large gathering of African Americans, I could set an imaginary timer to the time that the event would actually start compared to the advertised time. If a church musical was slated to begin at 7:00 PM, I would expect to not hear the welcome address until 8:15 PM. I grew up in a diverse school district and became quickly annoyed with my own parents when I had to make early band rehearsals, as well as Saturday rehearsals for school musicals and choir concerts. The humiliation did not only come from the disdain I received from school officials and classmates who had to wait for my entrance, but also the thought that I may inherit this problem once I reached adulthood. Can you remember the last time someone was late to a mutually agreed appointment with you? How did you feel? What was the excuse?

My experience in the military has not only brought negative feelings to this term, but has now encouraged me to despise a belief that I should be dysfunctional based on a racial identity. I will not accept this as being a badge of Black honour because there is no honour when you do not convey a sense of responsibility. A reason I despise CP time is that though a percentage of Black people take part, it affects those of all nationalities. When a Black American is late while being employed by a local courier service, it affects the Hispanic American who had a deadline. When an African American is late picking up his child from the daycare center, the African American teacher is now late caring for his own family. When you are late to an interview, the Asian American supervisor will not likely hire you for the position.

Though I may have a negative feeling toward the perpetuation of Black people being late, I have seen that some wear this as a badge of honour. You can expect those that include comedians and rappers to joke and portray being late as something that is accepted as being a part of the Black experience. Kanye West's lyrics tell you, "You should be honoured by my lateness." Ronald Walcott wrote, "CP Time actually is an example of Black people's effort to evade, frustrate and ridicule the value-reinforcing strictures of punctuality that so well serve this coldly impersonal technological society." The problem is not with the comics, lyricists, writers, or any other entertainers bringing undiscovered cultural idiosyncrasies to the main stage because I understand that art imitates life. However, rather than allowing entertainment, in any form, to dictate your life it would be best to allow life to replicate pride.

J.L. King wrote an entire book about the common perpetuation of Black people being late in his book *CP Time: Why Some People Are Always Late*. The stories that are displayed throughout the book will take you on a ride of pure shock and embarrassment. In chapter five Mr. King writes the following:

My best friend, a human resources director, shared with me that his company, a social service agency on the south side of Chicago, has three hundred employees (99% African American).

According to my friend, the number one reason that he has to terminate employees is due to them being late. The company's handbook clearly states: "Dependability, attendance, punctuality, and a commitment to do a good job are essential at all times. Excessive occurrences of absenteeism severely affect the functioning of programs. Disciplinary action may include oral, written suspension or termination.

I believe in the notion of receiving a full day of pay for a full day of work. From the time I was twelve years old pushing a lawn mower within a two-mile radius of my home in an effort to buy Tommy Hilfiger backpacks and Cross Color jeans, I have equated time spent with money earned. As a business owner and employee, I also see the benefit to increase productivity. To be a person who is perceived as having time management skills you need to put prior planning into practice. Nothing is more upsetting to an employer/management than to consistently deal with someone who seems to always have an issue with arriving at the appointed time or requesting an exception to policy because of yet another crisis. For instance, if you are blessed to have children who happen to have behaviour problems at school, establish a contingency plan. This is a plan that you follow if the first one is set aside in the event that some- thing unexpected takes place. A contingency plan would include providing the school with numbers of close friends and family who may be able to make visits on your behalf. If you fail to plan, you ultimately plan to fail. Unexpected issues are bound to happen in anyone's life but relationships with your superior may become strained if you are constantly bringing issues without a detailed course of action.

With regard to being punctual about your various appointments and extra- curricular activities that include everything from hair appointments, picking up your child (or children) from school or the babysitter, and returning from your lunch break within the parameters set by the organization that gives you the ability to pay for your necessities, why do you refuse to be on time? Is this based on the thought that you will do everything in your power, at all cost, to prove that you, like Frederick Douglas and Charles Drew, are authentically Black? Do you believe that your disregard for others and the lives they lead shows how important you are in a world that does not bow to you the way you feel justified that it should? If you respond to these questions with a resounding *yes* then I suggest that you understand that if your superiors, co-workers, and subordinates were asked whether you were considered professional then you would receive a resounding *no*. No matter how glamorous it looks to be "fashionably" late on television, it is not. Success won't ask whether you have arrived, it will only state that your time has come.

The idea that you possess the dark gene of the human race, which provokes you to feel that you supersede time constraints, is one that will leave you confined. You will be confined by what you think about yourself. Tom Burrell in his book *Brainwashed* speaks about this when he says, "I've experienced race- based lack of self-esteem first-hand. I know that it was not based solely on low income or poor education. As upwardly mobile as I was, that sense of lack was right there, climbing every rung of the ladder of success right beside me. Over time, I've learned that the root of the problem wasn't what was being done to me —it was what I'd been brainwashed to feel about myself." When I do not like something about myself or find that someone else does not, I have a past that triggers a response of pure indignation and rebelliousness in attempting to justify what I do. If you find yourself saying things or acting out in a way that shows this kind of response I urge you to stop—today.

This brings me to the topic of the side hustle. This term refers to a person who is paid to do a certain job but instead spends time at work in order to take care of personal business or endeavours. Many of us have seen this when co-workers promote a cosmetic line but will rarely turn in a scheduled report in a timely manner. Another example is the personal assistant who moonlights as a cosmetologist and books appointments instead of scheduling conference calls or corresponding with business associates. There is no excuse for this behaviour or level of *substandard dependency*. It is substandard dependency because the person who has hired you to perform a function that contributes to the greater good of the organization can no longer depend on you to be 100 percent present because you feel that, "You gotta do what you gotta do." This is not a reason for your behaviour but rather a crude and thoughtless excuse. Benjamin Franklin once responded to an employee who always seemed to have an excuse that "I have generally found that the man who is good at an excuse is good for nothing else." Begin to conduct yourself so that your weight in integrity, through punctuality, outweighs any trifling tendencies.

My hope for you is that you learn to schedule your time intelligently.

WHAT CAN I DO TO BECOME BETTER?

The next time someone is late meeting you for a scheduled appointment, don't just get upset. Think about why it bothers you so much. Think about the other things in your day that won't go right because the person is late. Remember the reasons so that you don't make a habit of giving that feeling to anyone else.

1. _____

   _____

   _____

   _____

2. _____

   _____

   _____

   _____

3. _____

   _____

4.

5.

Assessment #5

YOU DO NOT UNDERSTAND NETWORKING PRINCIPLES

Associate yourself with people of good quality, for it is better to be alone than in bad company.

—Booker T. Washington

When I started several different ventures I was given the advice: "People have to know you exist." I made sure I found the individuals and groups that would benefit from what I was attempting to accomplish. My first course of action was to attend a networking event sponsored by a local production company that catered to African American professionals. After I arrived promptly with a sleek messenger bag filled with brochures, business cards, and a laptop, I soon realized that I was one of the few who were there to actually network on a business level. Once I made my way around the room, leaving brochures at every table and engaging in conversations about my business, I began to scan the room. Instead of business cards being exchanged, alcoholic beverages were. Instead of reaching out to ensure the success of those who had come to take part in a "networking" event, there was a sense that the majority of those in attendance were there to size up those not in the outwardly professional demographic. Instead of gleaning advantages from those who had made great strides in the corporate world, a few individuals decided that it was more beneficial to remain isolated for fear of reprisal.

The fear of being seen as a brown-noser is something that I have been aware of. As a teenager, I had a chance to work at a local McDonald's. McDonald's gave me skills that I use to this day, both personally and professionally. During my employment, I was chosen to attend a pep rally sponsored for the organization. Attending the rally were those ranging from crewmembers to regional managers. A shift manager from my location became aware of a senior level manager, but rejected the idea of approaching the individual even though it would have helped his career.

Proper networking is used to lower the stress of the hiring process. If I take your resume on face value it is my duty, as an employer, to test that resume from all angles. That is also referred as doing *due diligence*. However, if a trusted peer suggests your name to me, regardless of who else applies for my openings, there is a higher probability that I will consider hiring you. Throughout my adult life, I have heard the saying, "It's all about who you know." I would take this a step further and suggest that *it's all about who knows you*.

If you were to walk into an interview, I believe that your level of confidence would be exponentially elevated if you were personally referred rather than your application being one of the many pulled from the company's job board. This is one of the purposes of networking. A December 15, 2012 article written by Michael A. Fletcher in *The Washington Post* cites Deirdre A. Royster, a New York University sociologist, who writes, "It is surprising to many people how important job networks are to finding work. The information they provide help people make a good first impression, get through screening and get hired." With this information, you may wonder why anyone would do that for you. Why would anyone suggest your name for a position that you did not know existed? The answer may just astound you. In many companies there is a "finder's fee" for bringing quality personnel into the organization, a practice that was used by the United States Army.

The fallacy of networking comes into focus when you rely on someone who talks as though they have certain knowledge of a particular company and offers empty promises. You need to make sure that the person really can help your career. Also, the way some individuals network is often nothing more than time wasted. For example, in the beginning of one of my first business ventures, a store that sold fraternal regalia and multicultural artwork, I ensured that my name and that of my business was on the lips of every potential customer. I did this by frequenting luncheons, mixers, and popular networking events. I was frustrated, to say the least, when I walked into a well-attended event at an established eatery in the city with brochures, flyers, and business cards in my briefcase. I was stepping out with shined shoes and a fresh shave, eager to make the advertised connections. What I found were masses of tipsy professionals who had not ever thought of exchanging contacts with the likes of me. Then there were the young women looking for a sponsor. The candidates had fresh shoes from Aldo, Kenneth Cole belt buckles, coach wallets, and were conspicuously flashing key chains bearing Mercedes and BMW emblems.

Remo Butler pointed out in *Why Black Officers Fail* that "while in a perfect world mentoring should transcend race, the reality doesn't match that ideal." In a post-Obama, world it is still not a common sight to see a corporate executive of a particular color or ethnic background mentoring someone of another ethnicity. I have personally sought out mentors of all backgrounds because I recognize that the business world is not homogeneous. One such mentor had an open dialogue with me about this observation. He told me that it goes to what you are familiar with. For instance, if I am a Senior Budget Analyst for a large firm, and I happen to be of Asian descent, it will be easier to mentor someone of similar appearance and background because in the mentee's mind he could easily be a younger brother or cousin from the neighbourhood or he might worship where I worship.

Networking makes you realize that you must actively be engaged in obtaining a position. Strangers, friends, and family who complain of not being able to find a position with a company often approach me. I often refute their claims by asking what specifically they are doing, or not doing, to allow that to be true. Now I will ask you. What are *you* doing *now* find a position? Filling out the occasional application without any follow-up or browsing newspaper classifieds are not good ways to find your dream position. When I find myself without employment (yes, even I experience this) I become a machine. Being a machine involves editing my resume and having it reviewed, creating accounts (Career Builder, Indeed, and Monster, for example) to search job boards and blast my resume to Human Resources departments, and reconnecting with individuals I have met previously in the field that I am interested. These are people I have met at job fairs that I have attended, personnel that I have built relationships with while employed with a previous company, and even peers in the industry or from school/training.

When you finally get the nerve to attend your first networking event, you must remember certain things to capitalize on your experience. Being prepared is a must. That includes arriving with the necessary materials. Business cards are the standard for this type of function but if you are not able to secure them ensure that you arrive with writing material that is professional in nature. This does not mean scrap paper, napkins, or mechanical pencils.

You also want to ensure that you remain genuinely interested and are, in return, interesting while remaining truthful. I have had a negative experience with this within the last year. I was invited to attend an industry (movie and film) networking mixer in North Hollywood at the W Hotel with a close friend who was expanding his business. If you have ever been to Hollywood, California or even heard about this seductive city, you may already know that there are a host of characters who call it home. That night in particular my friend and I met an individual who was dressed conservatively yet fashionably and maintained an atmosphere of respectability. While speaking to this young man red flags began to rise. For instance, he would describe his impressive business dealings, but when asked about a business card he responded that he did not have any. When asked about his projects he gave impressive statistics and investors but could not provide the intent or updates of the projects. I excused myself and researched him quickly via Google.com. I quickly saw that he was not the person he projected himself to be and soon rescued my friend from further dishonesty. Do not be this person no matter what you may feel about your sense of inadequacy. People have lost their jobs because they have lied on their resumes. Sooner or later your lie will come to the surface.

Like most other productive citizens, I keep a close ear to the reports about the U.S. and global economies and understand the current state. The recession is real, though it does not have to be *your* reality. Stocks will rise and fall, economies will grow, and large companies will default. All of it has an effect but don't allow that to discourage you from getting what you need and desire. You are not networking for the thousands of jobs that you heard were just shut down but rather for one job. The one job that you can and will excel in is still avail- able. The one job that you will do your due diligence to obtain is still available. That's the one job that will add to your life and to your bank account.

WHAT CAN I DO TO BECOME BETTER?

It has been said that it is a good rule to never eat alone. Invite someone from your department to eat lunch with you this week whether it is a subordinate, co-worker, or supervisor. Use this time to learn more about what's happening in your department and how it can affect you. If you don't have a job now, find someone to have lunch with who can help you in your search for a job.

1. _____

_____

_____

_____

2. _____

_____

_____

_____

3. _____

_____

4. _____

_____

_____

_____

5. _____

_____

_____

_____

Assessment #6

YOU HAVE A SENSE OF ENTITLEMENT

No one asked me to be an actor, so no one owed me. There was no entitlement.

—James Earl Jones

It saddens me to think that the gruelling labour that was forced on our ancestors would give birth to individuals who feel that work is not required for advancement. This also goes for those who believe that they don't have to continue doing the things they did to receive a position. The sense of entitlement in the United States has become progressively worse during the twenty-first century. Entitlement comes in various forms and I have encountered Black people who feel they deserve for one or more of these reasons. Some people think because they have achieved a certain position or rank in an organization they have a right to certain things. Some people believe their color renders them a high-valued commodity. Others base their feelings of entitlement on who they know or even on who they think knows them. This level of arrogance can distract people from their daily duties, and it can negatively affect how they are perceived in the workplace.

Whenever we read through biographies of various corporate executives, you and I can notice how they praise hard work and state that without it they would not have had the opportunity to rise to their current heights. Today Black people can see this in the person who has the highest position in America— President Barack Obama. No one, regardless of his or her political affiliation, can dispute that this man has worked his way from Columbia University, Harvard Law School, being president of the Harvard Law Review, working as a civil rights attorney and teaching constitutional law at the University of Chicago Law School—all of which he did before he entered politics.

Shortly after his 2008 victory, many Black Americans spoke of now being able to tell their children what is possible without hesitation. I also shared in this newfound symbol of possibility for my own son who was at that time a toddler. Though the position of president is revered (and I definitely think there is nothing wrong with that), I want you to know that the process a person goes through to reach that position is also one to be honoured and appreciated. There are too many of us who resent the process that placed us in our positions; that resentment can have a few effects. The effects can range from wanting to forget the process, which doesn't allow us to remember those days when super- sizing a meal was a luxury or thinking that we are too good for certain jobs because of what we have had to endure to be where we are.

I believe that you will have the position that you are destined to obtain. If you need a cheerleader or a fan, you have one in me. I say that so that you know my intent in this chapter is anything but dream killing. When I first entered the Army as a private I was in awe of the power and position of a company commander, which was held by someone of the rank of captain. I relished the idea while even writing my name with the prefix CPT (where no one would see it of course). I still had that dream while I cleaned toilets as a private first class. I set my aspirations on Captain as I was overlooked and challenged daily as a specialist. I kept my eye on the prize while I began to take on leadership roles as a sergeant. I ate humility and bathed in struggles as a newly commissioned officer and on the day I was told that I would be pinned captain and assume my first unit all I could say was, "Roger that."

It is important to know that I didn't become a Captain just because I wanted to be one. I saw what the steps were to get there. I made sure I did each job along the way to my very best, no matter what that job was. I made sure that I presented quality work so that people around me could be as proud of me as I was of myself. I worked at becoming what I dreamed of being. No one will make your dreams come true; only you can do that.

Entitlement is a tricky and sordid thing. While you are reading these pages you may think to yourself, "But I deserve a better job." or "He doesn't under- stand that everyone can't be like him." I beg to differ. Dreams are not given but rather taken by the throat. You can tell me all day what you deserve but that won't make it so. My great-grandmother, who I called Granny, deserved the world in my eyes. She was one of fourteen children, was married to an unfaithful man, worked as a domestic worker by cleaning for white families (the norm for that period), and took in her grandchildren during times when their parents were "finding themselves." You could not and cannot tell me that the sweet woman who cut my vanilla ice cream with a butcher knife and introduced me to coffee at eight years of age was not deserving of the most prestigious of honours. However, someone with her background, at face value, would not be offered a position at any company where I serve as the head of the hiring department.

There is something to be said about you if you are a person who feels that because you have completed certain degrees, programs, or certifications that you are "a shoo-in." Having the experience of being on both sides of the desk, I can assure you that if you possess a degree from a highly-ranked university and wear tailored clothes from your beautifully adorned head to the bottom of your red bottomed feet with just a hint of a designer fragrance and treat the inter- view as though I should have laid out a red carpet for your aura with consistent name dropping that does not apply to the position, it will not go in your favour. If you are followed by a gentleman with not-so-fresh waves due to the fact that he doesn't have enough money for a haircut, wearing a tie with a short-sleeve shirt, having shined his old church shoes with a Blue Magic shine—but he possesses punctuality, humility, and a desire to learn and excel, then you have just met your opponent who now has your position.

Growing up, my mother had the greatest influence on how I saw the world. She is the first person who placed in my mind that just because I was Black it was not synonymous with being dirty or inferior. She is also the first person I saw build a business from the ground up multiple times. I can recall times when her employees would gripe about how they wanted to do things that she did. For example, my mama would spend half of the day outside of the office and would come back with her freshly manicured nails carrying takeout. I would watch these scenes repeatedly the same way you watch an old "Good Times" episode, knowing that it was about to get very real, but everything would work out just in time for next week's episode.

My mother, being my mother, would sense this in what was her atmosphere and would say in a matter of fact way without turning her head or skipping a beat, "It costs to be the boss." When I first heard this I was in dismay that my mother could be so cruel and heartless to the very people who helped us have food on the table. However, it wasn't until some time later that I was allowed to go on these afternoon excursions with her and find out just what her life was like. She owned a few daycare centers but was frugal and self- reliant to the point of exhaustion, though she would laugh at the notion of being hospitalized for such a thing as exhaustion. What I found out was that my mama was *amazing*. Yes, she drove around in stylish SUVs, but they were used to transport children with schedules that conflicted with the AM and PM bus routes. Yes, her nails were done, but that was because she had broken them buying the groceries at one of those big box stores where you could buy in bulk. Yes, she brought in take-out food, but only because she had forgotten to eat in the midst of paying utilities, processing payroll, dropping receipts to the accountant, and strategizing how to keep her business afloat.

You may feel that you should have the corner office, extended lunches, expense accounts, or minimal manual labour, but there are some questions to consider. Does your experience warrant these perks and allowances? Does your role in the organization suggest that these are proper for you to complete your tasking? I do not ask these things to be pretentious, but only to suggest that the reason you do not have what you desire is because your current position does not warrant them.

When thinking about what you deserve, also consider what it may be like in that position.

Corporate executives, pastors of congregations, business owners, and high-ranking military officials will attest to the fact that with privileges come responsibilities, or as Bishop T.D. Jakes puts it, "Different levels come with different devils."

WHAT CAN I DO TO BECOME BETTER?

Take the next few moments and ask yourself what you would do if a twelve year old tried to tell you how to run your life, including your relationships and money. Would you be upset? What qualifications does the twelve year old possess to give you advice? Why would this bother you? Do you think he has enough experience? Then think about the times when you might be telling people with more experience how they should do things.

1. _____

   _____

   _____

   _____

2. _____

   _____

   _____

   _____

3. _____

_____

_____

4. _____

_____

_____

_____

_____

5. _____

_____

_____

_____

Assessment #7

YOU LACK PROFESSIONAL COMMUNICATION SKILLS

The most important thing in communication is hearing what isn't said.

—Peter Drucker

"It's not what you say; it's how you say it." There is no other quote that can sum up the ability to engage and maintain proper professional communication within the workplace. When you think about communication, what comes to your mind? You may reflect on the way you speak to colleagues in both face-to-face interaction and the telephone. Other communication topics include how you use body language to augment your speech, and how you receive certain gestures. Electronic communication, which is the standard for most businesses, along with text messaging is important for anyone communicating in this digital age. No matter what the type of communication you use, the main intent is to not make a permanent decision based upon a temporary emotion.

Speaking involves much more than just the words that are released from your mouth. Conversations are accompanied with hand gestures, facial expressions, vocal tonality, and body language. For instance, if I approached you and asked, "What are you doing?" would you be offended? Do you feel threatened? Is this a reason to approach the Human Resources department with a formal complaint? If I asked the question standing six inches from your face, with a harsh tone, my hands on my hips, my eyebrows raised and my head slanted slightly to the left would you feel differently? Again, it's all in the way you say something.

Culture has a great deal to do with what we feel is acceptable communication. In the military, it is imperative that leaders give direct orders in a manner that will not be misunderstood so they will be performed quickly by their subordinates. In families raised by "strong black women" (please see Assessment #8) the communication might be aggressive in nature, void of sympathy, and at times disrespectful.

When thinking about communication skills, make sure you do not over- look something that can be as powerful as anything that you have researched: the power of silence. The professional sense to know when words are superfluous is an outstanding skill that everyone from intern to CEO can learn and appreciate.

When considering telephone communication, remember not to make the obvious mistakes, such as not relaying a proper greeting whether you are making a call or accepting an incoming call. Also, give some thought to the tone in which you speak and whether you are able to listen effectively. All of these will make for a pleasant phone conversation and can help facilitate a potentially negative call. However, the way you end a call can have dire consequences if you are not knowledgeable. In my immediate family we often do not properly end a phone conversation by saying "bye" or any other common acknowledgement of good will. I did not understand that my family's practice is not the standard but rather the exception. I fought it for a time, feeling that the people on the other end were being needy or had too much time on their hands.

Electronic communication is in a world of its very own. In an email you want to be able to get your point across without having the recipient take offense to what you wrote regardless of whether it was factual or not. It is a good rule of thumb that you only send what you wouldn't mind being on the front page of the company newsletter. When you do receive an e-mail that is demeaning or untrue or that generally attacks your character (because you will), the first thing to do is to breathe deeply. Once you have gained your mental composure you want to address and confront the issues that were in the e-mail and not the person who sent it. This will show that you can keep your emotions under control, which management will appreciate. There are times when it will help you stay under control if you cc a person who is more senior to you and/or the person you're replying to. When doing this, be careful to not over-engage management or simply "put people on blast."

You knew it was coming. Talking Black, being fluent in Ebonics and being proficient in slang is a topic that is discussed in behind-the-door conversations, at water coolers, and in company-provided instant messaging, but is rarely mentioned out in the open. While writing this book, I would have various people of different ethnic groups and nationalities give me their opinion on the work I had completed to that point. One particular day stands out. I gave the draft to a white female to review for grammatical errors because she was attending college at that time. At the midpoint of her review she asked me if I had a problem with the verbs "are" and "is" and knowing where to place them. I reviewed the papers and realized that this mistake had been made a total of two times. However, instead of treating it like any other mistake she asked me if I had done this to attempt to bond with my readers by "talking black." Even now I am at a loss for words.

It is important that whether or not you are well versed in America's dark diction (Ebonics) or not, you need to ensure that you do not allow others to speak to you in anything other than Standard English. To do this would allow the perpetuation of the ignorant Negro. You may have already experienced someone of a different culture attempting to "talk Black" to you and if you have not, then wrap your hair and get ready. Do not tolerate the prevalence of co-workers attempting to identify with you. You are more than just an embodiment of a culture's stereotypical vernacular. Speak as though you have the mental capacity to comprehend standard office communication without feeling like an Uncle Tom. People attempt to relate to someone from a stand- point of ignorance outside of the workplace as well. This practice has been used successfully since the 1970s when advertising firms would change their marketing campaigns in an effort to attract and influence Black people by "putin' hot sauce" on their advertisements.

As the eldest of five children, I've been given many chances to teach. I have the luxury of having one brother, who we affectionately refer to as "Boonie". This name is not linked to anything that would suggest an embarrassing situation or reference to anything unsightly. This nickname is one of endearment that has been used generationally in my family. The name is used to such extent that it is how my sisters, close friends, and family can recognize an imposter down to the diction of the name. Though I have given you positive connotations in regards to his epithet, it should not ever be available in business settings.

A rule of thumb to abide by when you are conducting business for your- self or for someone else is that a swift response is a good response. When you are given the opportunity to excel in a leadership position you have to ensure that your section, unit, or team is working effectively and efficiently. Communication is a significant part of that. Being a leader involves you motivating people to do what you would have them to do. Being timely about your results means that you will have to convey ideas, updates, and problems between upper management and subordinates. The time frame in which you operate and communicate can be the difference between failure and success. I have been able to keep jobs and be promoted because of my reputation of giving swift and direct communication when an issue arises.

In a time of various modes of communication, such as fax, e-fax, email, snail mail, text messages, telephone calls, video teleconferences, and instant messaging you may feel overwhelmed by the pressure to stay connected constantly, but don't allow the pressure to paralyze you. If and when you do feel overwhelmed, take the proper steps to consolidate your modes of communication by only providing a maximum of three ways to be contacted. This does not show you being bourgeoisie but instead shows that you monitor specific lines instead of feeling the need to show your worth by the number of phones you are capable of answering. As a commander in the military I have not tried to show my superiors that I can use different communication systems because I know that particular information has been supplied via my resume. I have gained trust for being competent and effective by responding to their requests within the hour if during business hours and by the next day if I received a message after business hours.

When it comes to corporate/workplace communication I have had to realize and adjust to the fact that it is operated within the parameters of the Anglo culture. If you take a look at the statistics it is probable that you will also operate within that culture at some point in your career. It is indeed a balancing act to maintain your ways of operating and being able to assimilate to a different set of established practices.

I have had the advantage, once I proved myself as an asset to the organization, of discussing differences with co-workers; they were not aware. These differences include use of raised voices in an office environment. For some white Americans it is customary to operate in near-silence. One of the most apparent factors when I walk into a new office is the lack of noise. Another difference deals with the first greeting of the day. My experience has shown me that Black people from the South or southern Midwest are taught that if you walk into a room or see someone during the first part of the day, you speak and give the greeting of the day. A white instructor once told me a story about when he was a manager of a seamstress shop in Louisiana where the majority of employees where middle-age Black women. After his first few initial weeks he says that he was stopped by one of these employees and asked "Did I sleep with you last night?"

After he asked what the woman was talking about, she told him that might be the only reason that she could understand as to why he would not say anything in the morning—unless he just "wasn't raised right." I do not recommend that you confront your supervisor in this way, as it shows lack of tact. However, his experience shows how communication, or lack thereof, can be problematic in the workplace.

Unconscious racism on your part and that of your co-workers also needs to be considered.

The following Table that shows examples of verbal and nonverbal communications contrasts among some African American and some Anglo Americans. Dr. Orlando L. Taylor's *Cross-Cultural Communication: An Essential Dimension of Effective Education* from the Mid-Atlantic Equity Center that was revised in 1990 will assist with identifying possible problems.

Examples of Verbal and Nonverbal Communication Contrasts Among Some African Americans and Some Anglo Americans

Some African Americans	Some Anglo Americans
Hats and sunglasses may be considered by men adornments much like jewelry and may be indoors.	Hats and sunglasses are considered utilitarian as by men and as outwear to be removed indoors.
Touching another's hair is generally considered offensive.	Touching another's hair is a sign of affection.
Asking personal questions of a person met for the first time may be see as improper and instrusive.	Inquiring about jobs, family, and so forth of someone met for the first time is seen as friendly.
Use of direct questions is sometimes considered harassment, e.g., asking when something will be finished is like rushing that person to finish.	Use of direct questions for personal information is permissible.
"Breaking in" during conversation by participants is usually tolerated. Competition for the floor is granted to the person who is most assertive.	Rules on taking turns in conversation dictate that one person has the floor at a time until all of his or her points are made.
Conversations are regarded as private between recognized participants; "butting in" may seen as eavesdropping and not	Adding points of information or insight to a conversation, in which one is not engaged, is sometimes seen as helpful.

tolerated.	
The term "you people" is typically seen as pejorative and racist.	The term "you people" is tolerated.
Listeners are expected to avert eyes to indicate respect and attention.	Listeners are expected to look at a speaker directly to indicate respect and attention.
Speakers are expected to look at listeners directly in the eye.	Speakers are expected to avert eyes, especially in informal speaking situations.
Purposely including a minority person in group activities is seen as tokenism.	Including a minority person in group activities is seen as democratic.

Here are some basic forms of e-mail etiquette within organizations:

- Do not use e-mail to sell anything.
- Do not send: chain letters, offensive letters, mass e-mails, jokes, unnecessary pictures, and inspirational stories.
- Avoid using "Reply All" to prevent sending unnecessary e-mail traffic.
- Only make personal use of e-mail if allowed by the organization.

WHAT CAN I DO TO BECOME BETTER?

Go back through your previous e-mails and text messages and find one that you sent out of anger or frustration. What was the outcome of this message? Was it the best representation of who you are? How could you have sent the same message in a better way? How will you avoid making the same mistakes in the future?

1. _____

_____

_____

_____

2. _____

_____

_____

_____

3. _____

_____

_____

4. _____

5. _____

Assessment #8

YOU CONFUSE ATTITUDE FOR STRENGTH

If you don't like something, change it. If you can't change it, change your attitude.

—Maya Angelou

I can honestly say that I have hired based on attitude rather than skill and have also reaped the benefits of the same. All too often if you arrive at an interview with a chip on your shoulder, it will render the interview null and void. The company can train you, not change you. Not only can your attitude help you land the position that you desire, but it can also allow the employer to create a customized position just for you.

At times I see people carry a chip on their shoulders because they are young, Black, lacking funds, from the "wrong side of town," or resentful about some experience that they've had to endure. You cannot change the year you were born any more than the individuals who refer to you as a "kid" can change the fact that they were born decades before you. You can find your strength in changing your attitude. If you were to interview anyone within my vault, which consists of those I keep close to my heart, about my rock 'em sock 'em battle with my age, you can trust that I have had a great deal of experience with this. There have been multiple times when I have applied for a position by presenting a well-formatted resume that was valid, representing myself in telephonic interviews as though the CEO had given me the answers earlier, which led to receiving an offer letter.

Once I reported to orientation (ten minutes prior, at minimum), I've watched faces fall like the ashes on Pompeii at the fact that I was a young, almost childlike, Black version of what they were expecting.

The belief that some Black people, primarily women, have negative attitudes in the workplace and overall compared to other people has been relatively accurate in my experience. Our reputation is so bad that it has now become a commodity. The comedian Katt Williams pokes fun at this in his show "It's Pimpin' Pimpin'" when he says, " You done tried to return something to a Black woman at a store and she act like she bought you that shit herself personally and shit just embarrassing you in the store, just, *"Well what the fuck is wrong with it!"*

Because I have the privilege of being born, being raised, and existing as a Black individual, I hear how "strong" my friends and family are when they describe the outcome of situations that have ended badly. Because I do not allow my blackness to persist as a limitation, I hear a number of friends of different races describe and complain about dealing with Black people and their "sorry-ass attitudes." In the course of me working on this project I was even told that Black people's attitudes should be acknowledged and endured because of the past that we have.

I have issues with this thought because for someone to endure your negativity based upon the burden that your ancestors bore is unacceptable and a poor excuse for a substitute for reparations. Instead of having the notion that someone owes you a handout based upon a grievance that you did not personally endure, take advantage of the opportunity that your ancestors fought, suffered, and died for. You would not honour their legacies by allowing your rolled eyes and neck to roll you out of a job.

The first step in fixing a problem is admitting that you have a problem. Do you have an attitude problem? When we present ourselves with that question it is often answered with a resounding *no*. It is not so much that we lie to ourselves (though we do a good job at that) as we want to see ourselves in the most positive light available. There are signs that you do not play well with others, and these can be visible before you begin working for your desired company. On applications and résumés it is common to see references listed or at a minimum a message notating that they are available upon request. If you are not able to produce references—business or personal—then that presents a high inclination that you burn bridges as if it were your destiny and duty to do so.

Have you ever told someone in defense of your actions or words that you are a "strong Black woman/man"? If you have, please look inside and ask, what was the point of that declaration? It has been my experience that the people I encounter who make profound declarations repeatedly of the following: "I am the man of this house," "I am the H.N.I.C," "I am his wife," or "I am every- thing that you are attempting to be" are actually the individuals with the least amount of power.

There is a story of a C.E.O. who had the habit of sitting at the most far right chair in the boardroom, viewed as the "head chair." One uneventful day that same C.E.O. came and sat in a chair that was situated in the middle of the table. As the other members of the board filed into the room they all had an inquisitive look that suggested the C.E.O. must not have known where his place was at the table. Finally, a young executive sheepishly had a question for the C.E.O.

"Sir do you realize that you aren't at the head of the table?"

The C.E.O. grinned and effortlessly told the executive, "Anywhere that I sit is in fact the head of the table."

This story illustrates that when you have a certain authority or strength, it is not required that you boast or broadcast what you feel, but rather all that is needed is for you to rest in the role that you have assumed.

When you set forth a goal to become physically strong you must take many things into consideration. It is highly likely that you will not be able to lift every weight available during your first visit. It is also likely that you will need assistance on the proper techniques to maximize your efforts even though you have encountered heavy lifting before this time. However, with proper conditioning and adequate time your strength will increase, and you will become more productive during your sessions. In your life you have experienced events that would have driven others insane. It is important that because you were a survivor of violence, are raising a child alone, or have lost someone close to you that you don't equate that with possessing the proper skills that are necessary to operate in a new environment. Though your overall strength has been tested, there are certain muscles that are still in need of conditioning.

If you are currently employed or when you do make it possible to be employed there is something important to remember. Mr. Robert Carmona of STRIVE, during a hearing before the Joint Economic Committee on March 8, 2007, said "The other thing we try to get across to people is that the world of work is not a democracy. Rule No. 1, the boss is always right; rule No. 2, if the boss is wrong, refer to rule No. 1."

When you know your role it, at times, is easier to take your attitude out of the equation. For example, when your supervisor tells you that you have not produced the expected results in the area that has been assigned to you, it will serve as a way of your boss getting you to work harder or keeping you focused rather than you thinking that they are dissing you.

There is nothing wrong with being liked. Attending predominantly white schools for the majority of my life, I have had the experience of being well- liked in school. This reality was not always filled with joy and smiles. Any Black person who shares my experience in school, work, places of worship, and extracurricular activities knows how you can be deemed as an Uncle Tom of the month—or as the comedian Huggy Lowdown puts it, the "Bama of the Week." This critique can come from not being regarded as a Mandingo warrior to being feared in the copy room. Likeability, for some of you, is going to be a new territory because of how much we culturally perceive that we receive more or are respected more when we display negative attitudes by showing our asses on a daily basis. In Tim Sander's book, *The Likeability Factor*, he writes that "People who are likeable, or who have what I call a high L-factor, tend to land jobs more easily, find friends more quickly, and have happier relationships. Now believe that having a high L-factor isn't just a way to improve your life, it's a way to save it." Mr. Sanders is on to something; just think about the feeling you get from knowing that I, Asa Leveaux—*like you*!

There is a need for balance with regard to your attitude from your job hunt to job interview to your first day and beyond. In a conversation with an older Black woman, I brought up the difference between working with someone Black who is overly jovial and a Black person who has not notified her face that that she is in fact happy. She pointed out that no one wants to see fellow Black co-workers making a fool of themselves by offering to be the punch line of jokes or acting as a present-day minstrel show. My response to this was that no one wants to go to lunch with a grouchy and negative person regardless of his color. If you are in a small office or department and are not being asked to come to lunch or other gatherings, assess your attitude. You may be the highest paid Systems Analyst, the top sales agent, or the most beautiful creature who has ever graced a runway, but if your aura stinketh please take note of the people who are willing to be around you for an extended period of time. I can assure you that the number will soon dwindle.

WHAT CAN I DO TO BECOME BETTER?

Remember the last time you had a negative attitude toward a person or situation. How did this situation end? Was the ending good or bad? What could you do in the future to make such situations better? How could you show strength of character and a good attitude at the same time?

1. _____

   _____

   _____

   _____

2. _____

   _____

   _____

   _____

3. _____

   _____

   _____

4.

5.

Assessment #9

YOU PERPETUATE NEGATIVE STEREOTYPES

Applied for the job of rap-nigga, but I was over qualified.

—The Foreign Exchange

One of your main tasks while you are seeking a job is to reassure your potential employers that you do not display or have any traits that would cause trouble in their organizations. If you have been Black for more than a decade you are aware of stereotypes that are commonly associated with Black people in the workforce: lazy, undisciplined, poorly organized, incompetent, less-skilled, affirmative action hires, possessing bad attitudes, outspoken, rebellious, quick to blame management, dishonest, and quick to attack white peers, to name a few.

Dr. John U. Ogbu states, "Collective identity usually develops because of people's collective experience or series of collective experiences." (The Urban Review Vol. 36, No. 1). It is sad to say that stereotypes sometimes not only come from crass generalizations and bigotry but also the collective experience of a person or group.

I began my college career at Oklahoma State University in Stillwater, Oklahoma. I remain loyal to this school because this is where the Asa Leveaux that I am today was cultivated. It was very common to be one of the only, if not the only, Black student(s) in my classes (there were never more than three). It was an unspoken reality that I was the Black representative and that my actions and non-actions would greatly affect the idea of who and what a Black person at the collegiate level was. The reality conflicted with my truth. I make it a point to educate people of different cultures that I am not the chosen Black representative who will provide the inner secrets behind the uses of doo-rags, consumption rates of red Kool-Aid, or the idiosyncrasies of Tyler Perry movies. However, my role in diminishing long-standing stereotypes is a turbulent responsibility. Toure says in his book, Who's Afraid of Post-Blackness? that there are 40 million different variations of what Blackness is.

Malcolm Gladwell in his book Blink says the following:

> If you are a white person who would like to treat black people as equals in every way—who would like to have a set of associations with black that are as positive as those that you have with white—it requires more than a simple commitment to equality. It requires that you change your life so that you are exposed to minorities on a regular basis and become comfortable with them and

familiar with the best of their culture, so that when you want to meet, hire, date, or talk with a member of a minority, you aren't betrayed by your hesitation and discomfort.

Stereotypes hurt, especially when there is conscious collective thought about your particular group. In her book Why Are All the Black Kids Sitting Together in the Cafeteria? Beverly Tatum address this issue:

> Consider this conversation between two White students following a discussion about the cultural transmission of racism:
>
> "Yeah, I just found out that Cleopatra was actually a Black woman." "What?"
>
> The first student went on to explain her newly learned information. The second student exclaimed in disbelief, "That can't be true. Cleopatra was beautiful!"

Regardless of the times that I have read her book and come to this section, my soul that carries ancestral memories cries. It cries for all the times that I knew I couldn't.

Going into the year 2014 I see stereotypes of Black people being more relevant in the public domain. If you ask someone of a difference race or culture to explain what she would expect if she were to ever meet a Black person from the United States the response would be non-flattering to say the least. Until the early part of the twentieth century, the norm was minstrel shows with white actors in black-face portraying Black people as lazy, dancing coons. Even with everything that our people have accomplished we are currently portrayed in the mainstream as "Tacky. Violent. Ho." as described by Jeannine Amber in her "Real World" article in the January 2013 edition of Essence. Ms. Amber goes on to say, "From the all-out brawls on Basketball Wives to the grimy love triangles on Love and Hip Hop: Atlanta, reality TV has become a significant force in disseminating images of Black women to the viewing public." Has anything changed in the last 100 years that would honour the Black actors that had no choice but to play imbeciles and maids so that our young women and men could "keep it real"? Tarshia Stanley PhD., associate professor at Spelman College, sums up the issue this way: "This message can be particularly detrimental for young women of color who will be entering the workforce already fighting the stereotype that they're angry Black women about to go off."

I have dealt with stereotypes and the prevalence of what is portrayed about Black people longer than before I can remember. When you grow up in Oklahoma, in your childhood you are indoctrinated with cowboys, the Trail of Tears, and the Land Run. I loved everything about what I was being taught and I thought it was fascinating to hear how my state had begun and the lives of those on the frontier. I felt, however, that I was removed from the history. I felt this because no one ever referred to anyone of color during the lessons. One day, in kindergarten, I came home and told my mama that I wanted to be white as she gave me my weekly haircut. I remember her pausing without saying anything for a few minutes. When she asked me why I wanted to be white I simply told her that all cowboys are white and that Black cowboys do not exist. The experience that I received after that was the spark that lit the fire in my mind and my little Black-boy heart. That same week she drove me to the public library and showed me how to find books about people like Bill Pickett, Nat Love, and Mary Fields. That day I learned that Black people are everywhere and I was blessed to be among the many.

There are various stereotypes that go beyond those that I have listed. When it comes to searching for a position the list becomes longer. For instance, I have known or witnessed Black people listening to morning radio shows so that the station can pay their bills rather than using that time to search Craigslist.com, Monster.com, the classifieds, or anything productive that would better their situations.

The stereotype that I see most often is Black employees, and subsequently their friends, blaming others for their shortcomings when they are fired or at risk of losing their jobs. An example of this is a line from Kanye West's "I Heard 'Em Say" from his Late Registration album when speaks of his young cousin: "His job trying to claim that he too niggerish now/Is it cuz his skin blacker than licorice now?/I'm sick of it now."

In the book How to Make Black America Better, Tavis Smiley explores the notion of thinking Black when hiring for day-to-day needs.

For some areas in our lives, thinking Black is automatic. When we want soul food, a good barber or beauty shop, or place to worship, we know where to go. Plenty of Black people take our cars to a Black mechanic, regardless of whether he has his own shop or is replacing parts beneath a shade tree in his Back-yard. But more often than not, we don't take thinking Black to the next level. We don't put diligence into supporting Black stockbrokers, lawyers, agents, doctors, dentists, or web developers. We have ourselves convinced that in those arenas, the white man's ice is colder.

I would propose that if you are selling ice then you should ensure that your ice is just as cold if not colder than the "white man's." The point is that you need to present yourself, whether you are a financial planner or someone who is about to open a day spa, in a manner so that except for your face your race is not known. For instance, there have been far too many occasions where I have been given marketing material for a new business, personal résumés, or walked or driven by an establishment and automatically knew that it was from a Black person.

No matter the stereotype the common denominator of negative self-inflicted advertisements about Black people is the lack of pride. I am constantly amazed by personal and professional photography of Black people from the Harlem Renaissance until the 1970s. Whether I am looking at family pictures showing family functions or looking at the famous photograph that depicts five boys on the Southside of Chicago on the front end of the car in 1941 that is simply titled "Sunday Best," I ask myself constantly, what happened? Did individualistic freedoms put the ability to present oneself in a manner that conveyed worth on the proverbial back burner? Did the Black race become an imitation of what B.E.T. has the reputation of presenting so well?

WHAT CAN I DO TO BECOME BETTER?

Visit www.youtube.com and search for "minstrel show" and see if this is an adequate representation of who you are. At the same time, look at modern depictions of Black people. Are they adequate representations of who you are? How do you want to have people look at you?

1. _____

_____

_____

_____

2. _____

_____

_____

_____

3. _____

_____

_____

4.

5.

Assessment #10

YOU DON'T BELIEVE THAT YOU ARE AMAZING

Life has no limitations, except the ones you make.

—Les Brown

You are amazing! You are the beautiful, sun-kissed, dark-skinned, red-boned reproduction of an African ancestral line that is purely amazing. You only need to possess the testicular fortitude or ovarian audacity to make it so! The word amazing is defined by Merriam-Webster as "to cause great wonder or astonishment." You are by definition a great wonder on this great rock called Earth and you have the power to change the direction of your life today. I believe that the power I refer to is from the divine. Whether you call the divine God, Yahweh, Allah, or the Universe I believe that the divine does not make anything less than amazing. In my office I have boldly displayed a personal mantra that is written in Sanskrit, an ancient language and the primary language of Hinduism, that reads, om namah shivaya which translates into "I honor the divinity that resides in me." My intent is to keep this at the center of daily life so that I maintain the audacity to be amazing. Real recognizes real just as amazing recognizes amazing. I recognize this quality in you and believe that you are worthy of being called such. I believe that you can have the position that you desire. I believe that the company you are building will possess people of quality and conviction. I believe in you and not just your blackness. Is there evidence to convict you of being amazing? Does your walk display more than just swagger? Does it instead have a sense of purpose that can extend to corporate boardrooms and corner cubicles? Your ability to acknowledge and build upon the amazing that was conceived in you is made apparent by your finishing this book. In no way am I suggesting that this book alone will make you amazing, instead your desire to become better will eventually make this book null and void. You will see that there is a direct correlation between you being amazing and striving for excellence; one complements the other. Your evidence is set before peers, potential employers, and prospective partners in a way that brings the story of our heritage to light without the need of a Spike Lee film. Your heritage, whether you reside in London, Detroit, or Sao Paulo, was conceived in Africa, purified in endurance, and made relevant with your daily example.

I will now present further evidence. You are still here! The movie, *The Color Purple*, is well known and has become a cultural classic among many Black people. It stars Whoopi Goldberg, Danny

Glover, and Oprah Winfrey and is quoted often in Tyler Perry stage plays. There is a scene toward the end of the movie where after a climatic exchange across the dinner table the main character, Celie (Whoopi Goldberg), leaves the farm and man that have caused her years of strife and turmoil. As she is leaving Celie proclaims from the back of the vehicle to her husband, Albert (Danny Glover), that, "I'm poor, black; I might even be ugly, but dear God, I'm here. I'm here."

Though you may not be poor and most definitely not ugly, you are here. In spite of everything you have gone through from abuse to abandonment to feeling like you can't catch a break to being let go from your last position, you are still here. I believe that as long as you take pride in everything you do, there is no stopping you. Take pride in every written and telephonic conversation. Take pride in how you present yourself when business is to be conducted. Take pride in the color that creation has clothed you. Because you are here, in living color, I believe in your ability to make the most of every skill, degree, and stumbling block, so that your stepping stones place you on the level you were destined to dwell.

When you see a large tree that provides support and shade to many, remember that everything the tree is was once all in a seed. The same thing goes for you. Everything that you are meant to become lays dormant within you. With certain conditions and nourishment you will bloom. This book was meant to prune you so that you grow in a focused and precise way. I now give you the pruning shears to ensure your growth from this moment forward because as Jonas Salk says, "Our greatest responsibility is to be good ancestors."

The goal is to make your amazingness evident to others. The three ways to do this are through your reputation, resume, and references. I believe that your reputation can take you further and can directly affect your resume and references. Your reputation goes back to what you learned when I discussed networking principles. Your reputation is vital to your future success.

I have been blessed to meet many people in different industries, including event planners. One of those event planners sticks out in my memory because of his reputation. He is known in the city he operates not because of the fact that he graduated college, was successful within a Fortune

500 company, has a beautiful family, or has past successes as an event planner. The thing that I hear often when this person is brought up in casual conversation is how he does not pay his talent on time if at all. It is important to remember that you could have a million things that you have accomplished to standard, but if you lack in an aspect of your character then your certifications are null and void.

I am intentional about the positivity that I allow in my life. I am a part- time social media junkie, though my circle of friendly influence is relatively small on those various sites. We are products of our past experiences, and what we surround ourselves with including websites. There is a saying that if you show me your friends I will show you your future. I would add that if you show me your browser history I can predict your height. I dare you to take this challenge of going to your browsing history and doing an assessment of what you find. Does your history reflect your goals or does it mirror a past that you would rather not be joined to.

My amazingness is transmitted to me on a daily basis. I surround myself with people, messages, and quotes that inspire me to do what I once thought impossible. Whether I am at a stage where I am climbing the corporate ladder one pull and one step at a time or fortifying my vision to create my own ladder, I have support that is amazing. I do not know everyone that I reap these benefits from. For instance, I was blessed to find Les Brown on Facebook and am inspired by his posts. To give you an example of the beauty of this man's words, here is what he posted today:

You were born to win. Use your energy to find solutions instead of blaming yourself or others. Let go of your excuses, and don't give yourself a pass. Take responsibility and ownership for your life. You are greater than your circum- stances. You have the power to put your life in a different position. Remind yourself that you are intelligent, talented, and greater than anything that you have gone through! Tell yourself …"It's time to make a change!" Move forward with faith and confidence, and firm determination to live your dream because it's your destiny. The world is waiting for you. You deserve!

We have been amazing from the days of being referred to as niggers, to the days of being coined colored, to the present use of our current identity as

African Americans/Black People. While you hit the pavement and the World Wide Web searching for a position that you are qualified for, it is important that you walk with confidence and convey a demeanour that expects good things to come with every step taken. Expect that your color will serve as an asset to diversity rather than a stain on a whitewashed corporate world. Though your blackness is intertwined in divinity it is not the totality of your success. You are beautiful, intelligent, qualified, competent, and beneficial to any organization that believes in your potential.

Make being amazing your new normal. All of us have an existence that we can rate as normalcy. For some normal is catching the train each day to do what must be done, for others normal may be receiving rejection letters and "no" at every corner they turn, and for a few of us normal is the manifestation of minute-by-minute perfection. You have the power within yourself to choose how your life will unfold. I am an advocate for the bestselling book *The Secret* by Rhonda Byrne and a believer in the law of attraction. The law of attraction states that, "Everything that's coming into your life you are attracting into your life. And it's attracted to you by virtue of the images you're holding in your mind. It's what you're thinking. Whatever is going on in your mind you are attracting to you."

To be Black is to be amazing. I had an ah-ha moment with regard to this by watching Oprah Winfrey's Legends Ball. Oprah Winfrey honoured Black women like Maya Angelou, Naomi Sims, Dorothy Height, Leontyne Price, and Cicely Tyson for having paved the way for her and others with a three-day "living celebration" of love in the details. There was a poem by Pearl Cleage titled "We Speak Your Names" that embodied the purpose of the event. Your new normal is not to only present yourself as an amazing candidate at a job interview, but to also pave the way for other Black women and men who will celebrate the ways that you have made for them and the trials you have endured, on their behalf, along the way.

Have the courage to be amazing so that this book may become obsolete.

WHAT CAN I DO TO BECOME BETTER?

You are alive and completing a book at the same time! This life understands that you have more to offer and so it is refusing to let you go. Because you are amazing what will you do with your tomorrow?

1. _____

_____

_____

_____

2. _____

_____

_____

_____

3. _____

_____

_____

_____

4. _____

_____

_____

_____

5. _____

_____

_____

_____

Buried Treasure

We, together, have come to the intended destination. You have read and understood that the reasons Black people are not hired are not always from outside factors. Those factors do not always include the propensities of a premeditated racist or possess a "freakonomic" of the name that you were given or the heritage of the enslavement of a race of beautiful dark-skinned people. There are times, more often than not, that we desire to be perceived as diamonds while not allowing ourselves (in our coal states) to let the pressure of determination and hard work to transform us into gems. We want so much to be treasured but have we buried our most valuable gems?

I wrote this conclusion in February, the month when Black people in the United States and other parts of the world celebrate Black History Month by reflecting on accomplishments of our people that are often not acknowledged in mainstream academia. However, since I was a child I have been inundated with the success of those who are no longer in the land of living and for some time have questioned the actual motivation behind the celebration. Do you not want to make yourself better, hearing about the struggle of Charles Drew? Are you content with mediocrity once you read the speeches of Marcus Garvey? Do you continue to believe that your future is in direct correlation to how big your ass is when you learn about the gross display of Sarah "Hottentot Venus" Baartman?

This book is meant to be a part of the pressure that will turn you into a gem with shine and clarity. You have learned to respect not only others but also, and most importantly, yourself. If you come to an interview, an appointment, or a job late because you're on "CP" time you are not paying honour to your culture but rather you are under the impression that only your agenda is important. You have read in the previous pages that compartmentalizing your life by the way you dress and present yourself is not a sign of selling out but an explicit display of your maturity. The fact that you can receive your company's customers in an appropriate manner builds foundational workplace trust. I have expressed to you that regardless of your skill, talent, or ambition there are steps along the way for greater responsibility and compensation. You want to ensure that you don't abort the process that will take you to your promise.

I believe there is a level of greatness that you have not yet revealed to the masses. Because you have read these pages in entirety, you show that you have an eternal desire. Your desire to *know better* will now only be enhanced by your ability to *do better*. Your existence and value did not begin and end with slavery, and I dare you to make it so daily. Speak with the eloquence of Michael Eric Dyson. Ensure your appearance is impeccable like Tiki Barber's. Pursue the corporate ladder the way Ursula M. Burns has done. Take a page from the book of Command Sergeant Major Michele S. Jones and be so good that they can't ignore you. The Black treasures of today show us that excellence didn't die with Martin Luther King Jr., but that we can now shine on both sides of town.

NOTES

Why I Won't Hire Black People

Appendix A

Suggested Material

Suggested Reading

Black Faces in White Places by Dr. Randall Pinkett

Cracking the Corporate Code by Price M.Cobbs and Judith L. Turnock

The Happiness Advantage by Shawn Achor *Working While Black* by Michelle T. Johnson *The Slight Edge* by Jeff Olson

I Got My Dream Job and So Can You by Pete Leibman

The Harder We Run by William H. Harris Speech: "Unemployment" by Marcus Garvey

Suggested Websites

- Communication Techniques
  https://www.expressyourselftosuccess.com

- Corporate Image
  http://jillbremer.com/

- Success
  http://www.addicted2success.com

- Networking
  http://www.LinkedIn.com

- Resource
  http://www.careeronestop.org

Suggested Songs for Playlist

"Encourage Yourself" by Donald Lawrence

"Golden" by Jill Scott

"Smile" by Kirk Franklin

"Try" by Cooki Turner

"Closer" by Goapele

"I'm Walking" by Donnie McClurkin

"Alright" by Darius Rucker

"Push Yourself" by Rod Porter

Appendix B

Success Stories

Peggy S. Butler
12802 N.W. 38th Avenue
Reddick, FL 32686

My interactive tweet with author Asa Leveaux, prompted an invitation to be part of his controversial book, *"Why I Won't Hire Black People."* In keeping in step with the book's theme, I wrote a commentary titled *"Rules, Rituals and Gaffes of Job Interviewing,"* with emphasis on mistakes, African-Americans make when applying for jobs, and how to counteract those blunders.

Ask the typical African-American applicant, why they fail to attain jobs in Corporate America, and you are likely to hear a barrage of answers, ranging from the sublime to the ridiculous. Now go ask a Fortune 500 CEO, that same question and you'll hear an assortment of answers, so contradictory, it will leave you breathless. Why such varied responses? It's simple: Individuals of European origin base their response on myths, stereotypes and other subjective factors, in comparison to Blacks who live their lives entrenched in color.

What can be said about a race of people that has not been said before? Do we dare define African-American as a morsel of flesh, a mountain of humanity, a thunderbolt of patience? Courageous, proud, majestic, dauntless, we are all this and more.

Who else but African-Americans could have survived slavery, lynching and every tragedy imaginable and emerged victorious? However, like other ethnic groups, we too have a dark side. Among the barriers that impede our progress is the misguided belief, that our color prevents us from reaching the corporate boardroom.

Admittedly, there are thousands of cases, in which racism plays a pivotal role in the employment realm. However, it must be noted, that many applicants, fail to get jobs, because they don't adhere to the general rules of interviewing.

Now, before anyone starts ranting that these rules don't apply today, my response would be, really? Not surprisingly, these rules are as important today, as they were 30 years ago.

As a Black woman, I understand that it is easier to justify our failures using standardized racism theories, rather than taking responsibility for ourselves. Honestly, haven't we reached the point where it's time to retire the excuses, and face the fact, that no one owes us a damn thing? Not even a customary hello!

Thus, in reading this commentary, it is my hope that African-Americans will observe the Rules, Rituals and Gaffes of Job Interviewing, and vigorously pursue the American dream of life, liberty and happiness.

Peggy S. Butler

Rules, Rituals and Gaffes of Job Interviewing!

by Peggy S. Butler

It is a ritual every applicant dreads, the all-important interview. How you conduct yourself during those critical minutes, determine whether you are hired or rejected. To help job seekers survive this complex process, below is a list of do's and don'ts to be used before, during and after an interview.

Before

Do

1. Wear proper attire. For men that means a suit. Second choice is a shirt and dark trousers. Similarly, women are advised to wear suits (black or blue preferably) or a conservative dress. WARNING: Sistahs, many of us have a habit of squeezing into a skirt two sizes too small that accentuates the rear end. Avoid making this fashion blunder. The interviewer does not want to see anything that reminds him of Jell-O, shaking and jiggling compulsively. Moreover, young men, if you plan on wearing those baggy pants that hang below the waist, and show your underwear, forget it. No one is going to take you seriously dressed like a Lil Wayne impersonator. Getting rejected because you lack the proper qualifications, or have less experience than another candidate is discouraging but endurable. However, failure to get the job, because of your

sloppy appearance is entirely your fault. Don't forget: Judgment, whether fair or critical, is formed as soon as you walk in the door.

2. Arrive on time. Nothing turns an interviewer off quicker than an applicant who shows up late. To avoid this blunder, leave home 20-30 minutes early. And for those applicants, who conscientiously adhere to the CPT (Colored People Time) theory. Hey, come closer, there is something I want to tell you. In Corporate America, only one time is essential, the right time. So, forget, all that CPT mumbo-jumbo, because the interviewer certainly has.

3. To counteract nervousness, rehearse what you are going to say. Behaving like a reject from "Dumb and Dumber" won't win you any admirers. However, you may get a vacant stare from the interviewer. Comprende?

4. Anticipate what questions the interviewer will ask. If you're unfamiliar with this format, read books on various types of interviews. One document I recommend is *"The Everything Job Interview Book, 3rd Edition"* by Lin Grensing-Pophal.

5. Look, Sound and Act Confident. If you believe you will get the job, there's a strong probability you will. Now is the time to showcase your brilliance, so go for it!

6. Smile upon meeting the interviewer, and shake his/her hand firmly. Nothing sinks an applicant quicker than a frown and sweaty palms. Not surprisingly, Blacks are notorious for having frosty dispositions. So, practice smiling. What have you got to lose? A headache, perhaps?

7. Learn all you can about the company to which you are applying. If you want to make a good impression, show the interviewer you have done your homework. That means you must be willing to learn all you can about the company in question. Information to know includes: What the company does and what has been its growth pattern over the years.

Don't

1. Make a spectacle of yourself.

2. Fall to pieces, upon meeting the interviewer.

3. Don't panic. Although getting a job is the goal. It's not the end of the world.

During

Do

1. Look the interviewer straight in the eye. Failure to do so indicates nervousness.

2. Answer questions that require more than a yes or no answer. After all, no one likes an individual who is one dimensional to the point of ad-nauseam.

3. Be honest. If any inconsistencies crop up that demand answers, be willing to explain your position, calmly and intelligently.

Don't

1. Put your foot in your mouth.

2. Ramble on aimlessly. The interviewer does not want to hear about your neighbors impending divorce. Nor are they interested in that cold sore on your lip. So put a lid on it!

3. Criticize former employers. If you appear angry or bitter, the interviewer will pick up on your reaction and characterize you with the petty label. Remember, negativity can be detrimental in securing employment, so avoid it!

After the Interview

Do

1. When asked if you have any questions, make sure you have at least two. A no response indicates lack of interest.

2. Ask the interviewer when they anticipate making a decision.

3. Following the interview, write a thank you letter. This will make you stand out from the rest of the applicants, who may have omitted this important step.

Don't

1. Focus on the negative aspect of the interview. This will only lead to frustration.

2. Look sad, angry or dejected. A defeatist attitude indicates inferiority.

3. Forget to congratulate yourself for making it through the interview.

Remember: During an interview you are judged on your appearance, behavior and communications skills. Strive to create a positive impression that will convince the interviewer, the position was created just for you. Now, go out and get that job. Damn I'm good. Next!

Bio

Peggy S. Butler is a freelance writer based in North Central Florida. She has written for various magazines and Internet publications including Africana.com. and TimBook Tu. Moreover, Butler who lists collecting 60s memorabilia among her hobbies; writes news, features, sports and entertainment articles, as well as commentaries and humor pieces. Visit her website at peggysbutler.com or track her at Twitter.com/peggybutler647.

Peggy S. Butler

DEPARTMENT OF THE ARMY
FORT HOOD MOBILIZATION BRIGADE
BLDG 4228, 78th STREET
FORT HOOD, TX 76544

IMWE-HOD-HMB-HHD					31 December 2012

MEMORANDUM FOR RECORD

SUBJECT: Why I Won't Hire Black People c/o Asa Leveaux

1. As an HR Manager going on 16 years, I have had the opportunity to work for several Fortune 500 companies as well as the US Army and local State Government. Every organization has its own distinct personal culture based on its industry and environment. Corporate America has its own jagged ladder to climb and glass ceiling to break thru. The US Army has rules and regulations which govern a Soldier's every move. Whereas State Government is based on politics and the political reach of the State Representative or State Senator who holds your individual agencies purse strings.

2. Due to this dynamic of state government, if a State Representative or State Senator were to send you a letter requesting one of their district constituents be interviewed for an entry level position, there was really no saying "no". On one occasion, while interviewing for several entry level caseworker positions, I received several such letters from state officials. Along with my chosen interviewees, there was also a list of "political candidates".

3. As the day progressed with the interviews, several of the "political candidates" arrived to the interviews wearing less than professional attire. There were stiletto heels, low cut blouses, tight dresses, sagging pants, no tie or dress shirt, rows of earrings, lip ring, purple hair, and gym shoes. One interviewee I mistook for a client who I thought was waiting for an appointment with his caseworker. Now I do understand that some individuals may not own a suit or can't afford one (especially if they are unemployed). But to arrive to a professional interview in night club attire is unacceptable. It's seems as if our young people have no clear guidance of what is considered professional.

4. We now live in a time where style and class has now been replaced with "swag". You now see celebrities walking the red carpet in suits, baseball hats and sneakers. What was once casual wear has now become professional wardrobe. "Casual Friday" has now been replaced with everyday, khaki pants, jeans, and sandals. This is fine, once you are actively employed with the company and this is their culture (ex. Face book, Google... etc). But until that time, our African American young people need to raise the bar for themselves and make sure their work ethic, resume or application speaks for them, not the distraction of their clothing.

Lameka D. Grayson

LAMEKA D. GRAYSON, PHR
CPT, AG
Brigade Plans Officer

Joseph Ballard II, M.Ed.

2916 Snowdrop Drive, West Lafayette, IN 47906
(405)474-6702 ● jballard2010@gmail.com

December 4, 2012
Why I Won't Hire Black People
C/O Asa Leveaux

Dear Why I Won't Hire Black People,

I hope this evaluation finds you well sir. I just wanted to provide a brief assessment on the topic of "You do not understand networking principles". I will start begin by providing a little background of something I experienced while interviewing someone to be on the executive board of one of my student groups that I advise.

Well, one of my student organizations was in the process of electing new officers for their upcoming school year and one of the requirements was that each candidate participates in a fifteen to twenty minute interview with the current student officers, me, and other staff members within my office in order to move forward with the election process.

This student, who I will call Thomas due to FERPA regulations, came to the interview not dressed in business professional attire which was stressed many times to him by the committee to do so we gave him the benefit of a doubt and preceded with the interview. The interview was one of the worst interviews we had. When asked to describe himself, he really couldn't do it in the time allotted for it. I learned in my business administration class in undergraduate that when giving a "elevator speech" you are usually allotted less than a minute to describe yourself and he took three minutes to do that. Another thing that occurred was that he could not differentiate himself and did not have solid goals or initiatives coming in. When running for a leadership position, you must have solid goals and initiatives that you do that will improve the lives of the community in which you serve and this student was more concerned about the parties.

He also did not really try to reach out and network with other students in the organization and/or advisor for the organization to get an idea of our expectations as well, more importantly begin building up his network of support to help him be successful at this university which is essential as an African American, especially African American male at this predominately white institution to be successful.

Thank you for your consideration.

Sincerely,

Joseph Ballard II
Student Program Specialist/Academic Advisor
Purdue University

POOCH COATURE

Phone: (917) 474-2060 • Email: tamur@poochcoature.com • Web: www.poochcoature.com

Dear Inquisitive Minds,

When asked to write an excerpt to be included in "Why I Won't Hire Black People" I was elated. My 1st thought was, "wait a second, this has got to be going somewhere."

Beyond what I could have instantaneously fathomed, my next thought was, "this is going to be good." One thing was for sure, I definitely wanted to hear more about this ole black people jig. Two things were for certain, I knew that His-story was being told and our story needed to be told.

As a young black woman and entrepreneur I aim to excel beyond measure. I am learning to be my biggest fan and pray that I move past being my worst critic. The pressure of doing both simultaneously doesn't always have a positive outcome when combined. When I decided that I was going to be the face and the voice of my own company and brand it didn't come without careful thoughts. Can I do this? How would I get the resources to make this dream a reality? What would those resources be? Am I enough to dream a big dream and step out into that dream? If I took the plunge and risked it all, would I be ok with the outcome, whatever it may be?

My driving force behind seeking entrepreneurship was my dislike for Corporate America, the very place that gave me the fight to choose faith over my bad experiences. With boss' that sometimes overlooked my exceptional work, under-minded by undeniable talent or just didn't have the courtesy and professional class about themselves to treat me like an equal (Entitlement? Yes. Confusing attitude with strength? Perhaps). My greatest challenge in corporate America has been ending up on the battle ground of being misunderstood. From my dark mesmerizing skin tone to the city-southern twang that I picked up; somewhere along the way BETWEEN a black girl lost from Brooklyn, NY... AND the long dirt roads of southern hospitality, with a spicy draw that only a select few could appreciate, I found that I had been being groomed for the very place that I would despise the most, Corporate America.

In owning my own business I set out to defy all the typical rules of professional engagement or what many would deem the societal norm for doing business in Corporate America.

I left Corporate America groomed for success, because I was determined not to be on the denial list of candidates. I was going to show up to every interview, expose every opportunity, crash every website, talk to every person that God led me to or placed in my path until I figured out who I needed to become to own my power and succeed in this lifetime. My success came about because of who I was not, not who I immensely appeared to be. I did notice something special about me during my corporate America days. I never left an interview without leaving a lasting impression on the interviewee. The problem came in when I actually got the gig. I became comfortable very quick. I would show up 5 to 15 minutes late for an initial interview, but thought I was safe because I blamed it on traffic. After about 3 weeks to a month on the job I would run late and thought I was safe because I blamed it on traffic or pulled a Milli Vanilli and just blamed it on the rain! (Disrespectful of time? Absolutely). After days or even weeks of grueling training, I would get attention deficit disorder (ADD); sitting at a desk, in a cubicle reading scripts or just not being challenged caused me to misbehave. I couldn't help but daydream of clicking my feet like Dorothy and ending up in a land with my ToTo, far far away from paper, pens, ringing phones, a slow unstable elevator, a controlled 30 minute lunch and 2 insulting 15 minute chatty breaks, hating co-workers and all the misery love company bunch that tended to be older women living vicariously through me. I began to adopt sabotaging behavior. I began to justify my lack of giving 100% to an employer based on where I had hoped to be in the near future and even convinced myself that being at their place of business was interfering with my forward progression (Victim mentality? Discretionary). This behavior became my entrance and my exit, my stage left, right and center for my existence in Corporate America. And if I may keep it all the way real, I have always known that I was born to be great and do mind blowing things to the highest degree. I make no apologies about my journey to a better me, but rather identifying with the mentality I had while trying to fill the shoes of being successful while managing my blackness in corporate America.

In owning my own business, I understand the disparities of black people compared to our counter parts and some ideologies of the mentality of black people as a whole, based on an economic and social status. In my opinion, black people fall into two categories in association with Corporate America. They are either to corporate, in which they fall out of like with their black selves and may lose a sense of self to climb the ladder of success or due to the lack of planning and preparation others miss the window for creating opportunities for themselves, within a corporate environment.

As a business owner, I have spent time working through a lot of who I use to be and diving into who I am destined to be. You can't move into the new and improved until you move out of your own way and into the absolute truth. I will hire black people, but I won't hire the old me.

Sincerely,
Ta'mur Rasul
Designer

www.ingramcontent.com/pod-product-compliance
Lightning Source LLC
Chambersburg PA
CBHW060525100426
42743CB00009B/1436